Hart Westcombe

The Irish question; its essence, course, solution, and the issues it involves for Ireland and for England

Hart Westcombe

The Irish question; its essence, course, solution, and the issues it involves for Ireland and for England

ISBN/EAN: 9783337124489

Printed in Europe, USA, Canada, Australia, Japan

Cover: Foto ©Andreas Hilbeck / pixelio.de

More available books at **www.hansebooks.com**

THE IRISH QUESTION:

ITS ESSENCE, COURSE, SOLUTION,

AND THE

ISSUES

IT INVOLVES

FOR IRELAND AND FOR ENGLAND.

A MONOGRAPH

IN THE FORM OF

A LETTER TO THE PRIME MINISTER

BY

W. HART WESTCOMBE.

—Till TRUTH and RIGHT from VIOLENCE be freed,
And PUBLIC FAITH cleared from the shameful brand
Of PUBLIC FRAUD; in vain doth Valour bleed—
While AVARICE and RAPINE share the land.—*Milton.*

LONDON:

KEGAN PAUL, TRENCH & CO., 1, PATERNOSTER SQUARE.

1886.

GOD FOR HIS MERCY! WHAT A TIDE OF WOES
COMES RUSHING ON THIS WOFUL LAND AT ONCE!
        *   *   *   *

THAT ENGLAND THAT WAS WONT TO CONQUER OTHERS,
HATH MADE A SHAMEFUL CONQUEST OF ITSELF.
        *   *   *   *

NOW LEAN-LOOKED PROPHETS WHISPER FEARFUL CHANGE;
RICH MEN LOOK SAD, AND RUFFIANS DANCE AND LEAP,—
THE ONE IN FEAR TO LOSE WHAT THEY ENJOY,
THE OTHER, TO ENJOY BY RAGE AND WAR:
THESE SIGNS FORERUN THE DEATH OR FALL OF KINGS.

King Richard II.

PREFATORY NOTE.

THOUGH the present Monograph appears in the form of a Letter to the Prime Minister, nothing is farther from the mind of the writer than to convey the impression that the *matter* contained in it is to be regarded as of merely temporary, fleeting, interest and importance,—and therefore to be forgotten or neglected when we possess full knowledge of the " measures " now impending. On the contrary, the object of the Author has been—to bring into small compass the leading phenomena which must be studied, now *and in future*, by everyone interested in the solution of the Irish Problem. And although the Prime Minister of the hour is addressed, and his activity specially criticized,—yet the reader is requested to regard him as only *one* of a class of political nostrum-mongers with which these islands are likely to be afflicted for many a long year. May this little book tend to efface that pernicious class, and so shorten the days wherein we are to suffer adversity !

To

The Right Honourable W. E. GLADSTONE, *M.P.*

SIR,

  In common with many thousands of Her Majesty's You request "authentic knowledge." subjects I have read your extraordinary letter addressed to LORD DE VESCI, inviting "*free communication of views from the various sections most likely to supply full and authentic knowledge of the wants and wishes of the Irish people*";—and in common with some hundreds of them I have undertaken to comply with your request.

A most astounding request it is. In the first place, it seems to imply an abdication on your part of the elementary functions of statesmanship. The business of a steersman is—to steer,—of a responsible politician—to devise and carry out a policy. Again, I should have thought that the proper, the constitutional source of "full and authentic knowledge of the wants and wishes of the Irish people" would have been the hundred-and-odd representatives of the Irish constituencies "duly" elected a few weeks ago to serve in the Commons' House of Parliament, and elected on a plan designed and arranged by yourself. But once more, the passage I have quoted contains an ambiguity from which few of your public utterances on the Irish Question are wholly free. The ambiguity lies in the term "Irish people." What do you mean by the "Irish people"? Again, when you have got this knowledge, "What will you do with it?" How will you test it? What would you do, suppose the weight of evidence furnished by these "various sections" should lead you to make proposals (when you come one of these days to "settle" the Irish Difficulty) that would not commend themselves to a majority of the Irish members? If, for example, you should be convinced by the arguments of the Irish Defence Union, would you hold your hand, abandon office, abandon public life altogether —rather than march in step with the party which you once

B

described as bent on " stalking through rapine to disintegration and dismemberment "?   That you are in a difficulty is manifest.   Do what you will, turn where you may,—hemmed in—nay, more, *surrounded*—you see, I should imagine, difficulty—and ever difficulty.   The Irish Question you have made the question of the hour : it may hereafter be pronounced to have been, for England, the question of the century.

I can give " authentic knowledge," and I give it.
But you may fairly ask what "section" I represent.   I will tell you.   I represent by distinct and formal delegation the views of a small body of persons who are (1) professed students of the History of Nations, and of Politics, in the widest sense of the term ; who (2) have lived each of them for at least a quarter of a century in Ireland ; who (3) have lived many years in England (some, indeed, having been born on this side of the Irish Sea), and who (4) have material interests at stake in this business. The last consideration, however, weighs with them so little that it would not of itself have induced them to trouble you at present. But they are moved to do so because they are sincere well-wishers of all Her Majesty's subjects, whether English or Irish. These, then, are my sailing orders.—

First, then, —*you will fail*,
The first statement I am instructed to make is—and I may add, what is *absolutely certain* in this crisis of the history of (not only Ireland but) England is—what can admit of no manner of debate, is—that you, sir, are not destined to initiate now or at any future time a policy bearing ever so remotely even *in the direction* of a solution of the Irish Question.   We have examined your habit of mind and character, we have examined your professed principles,[1] we have examined your record—and we have pronounced this conclusion to be irresistible.

Passing over, for the present, the psychological aspects of the matter, and confining ourselves to facts that are past recall, I (speaking now and to the end in my own person) affirm that you have already—with the best intentions in the world—rendered the Irish Problem—on this side Revolution—absolutely *insoluble*.

[1] The difficulty we have encountered being not to *examine* your principles—*that* we are perfectly willing and competent to do—though *we* say it,—but to *find* them.

First, by a series of measures you steadily lessened the possibility of a solution of the problem; and then by a final measure you have scored a " lost ball " ; you have hit the problem, if I may so speak, clean away out of the region of things soluble by ordinary processes. And now, having rendered by the labours of many " days and nights " this momentous problem absolutely insoluble, you propose to solve it by a further and more complete application of the principles and methods that have rendered it insoluble ! Sir, your present activity will end in disastrous, dismal Failure. It can have no other issue.

In support of this thesis, and with the view of enlightening posterity, and also of bringing as many Englishmen as possible back, by God's grace, to a better mind than they have shown in making you Dictator and Saviour of Society, I will enlarge a little on this Irish Problem and on your relation to it. Before doing so, however, I premise three things :— *as I will now proceed to prove—premising only :—*

1. I will not be seduced into discussing any part of the subject *in detail*. My remarks shall, as far as possible, be *general*. That does not imply, as many people might imagine, that they will be *vague*. They will not be vague : they will be *comprehensive*. Mastery of detail is, *we are told*, your strong point; and mastery of detail is admirable when the subject of discussion is, say, the Greek verbs in $\mu\iota$. But mastery of detail may become in a statesman a very dangerous quality : it tends to obscure even to himself the possible weakness of *principle* underlying his measures; and it tends to bewilder a stupid people like the English into acquiescence, when acquiescence means wrong and danger and disgrace. —At the present time, for example, we read of nothing in the papers but a proposal—started by a distinguished Figure-man, and supposed to be one of those proposals that will be made by you one of these days—a proposal to expropriate the Irish landlords at the cost of adding £200,000,000 [1] to our National Debt. Now, many intelligent Englishmen, Able Editors and others, are aghast—but at what ? At the all-round *profligacy and folly* of the proposal ? Not at all : only at the prospect of our having *to find this enormous amount !* A side issue altogether. And some seem to think that the whole difficulty is settled when *(i) that I shall confine myself to principles;*

[1] More or less, and it makes no matter how much more, or how much less.

they are able to explain that certain Customs and Excise duties to be levied in Ireland will be ample guarantee for the interest; and many would be easy in their minds, could they but see introduced such blessed words as a " sinking fund," and "terminable annuities." Now the *fact* is (but you get at this by looking at the *principle* of the thing—not by fogging yourself at the outset in details): It would be better for England, suppose she wishes to exist as a nation, to pay £200,000,000 and fight campaign after campaign in order to *avoid,—prevent* the state of things that will immediately ensue on the disgraceful surrender implied in buying out the Irish landlords. The measure literally reeks of villany; but the difficulty with Englishmen is—*to find the money!* If the thing could be compassed for a million, they would not hesitate.[1] Well, the statesman who could propose and the community that could carry out such a measure are face to face with well-deserved disaster.—I will avoid details, then; my present object will be more completely attained by discussing *principles* and by sticking to *general* truth; it were easy in every case to give chapter and verse.

(ii) that my *wish and interest* is that the Question should be solved;

2. I (personally and representatively) have not the slightest wish that you should fail in your present undertaking. All my wishes, all my interests, as I have already intimated, point in the opposite direction. I am not a journalist; I am not a professional politician of any faction or school; I set small store by that greatest of earthly blessings—the franchise. But I am a loyal subject of Queen Victoria—though the profession of loyalty, it seems, is to *you* quite unmeaning: at least you decline to consider any difference as existing between two Irishmen of whom *one* asserts

---

[1] And some of them are beginning to swear roundly that we English *won't* find the money,—or rather (for we are first and foremost a *moral* people) that we *oughtn't* to find the money. For, don't you see (so argues a certain Earnest man,) the landlords have been getting rack-rents for centuries (especially, I suppose, those who bought property in the Encumbered Estates' Court in, say, the year 1879)—so that from financial and moral (especially *moral*) considerations we must refuse any indemnity on their being forcibly expropriated and banished. And that Ireland was rack-rented is *proved* by the enormous reductions in rent made by the Land-Commission.—That is, the *fact* that a man *has* been robbed proves that he *ought* to have been robbed; and his having been robbed once is ample proof that he *ought* to be robbed again!—Truly we *are* a moral people!

that he is loyal and *the other* boasts that he is disloyal. (By the way, are both loyal or both disloyal?) Anyhow, to Englishmen and Irishmen alike I wish well—σφιν εὔφρονέων. But neither my wishes nor interests, nor prayers nor vows will serve to avert this signal, this *final* Failure !

3. I have always refused, I refuse now, and, no matter what happens, I will to the bitter end, refuse to discuss the question, wholly irrelevant as it is, whether you are actuated in what you do, by the purest motives, the best, noblest, most virtuous intentions. I freely admit that there is not a man in England to whom, *from his own standpoint*, the " General Confession " in the Church Service approaches so nearly to a mere form of words as it does to you. Nay, I will affirm that if you *could* use the formula of the Pharisee, you would be justified, *Te judice*, in " thanking God that you are not as other men." Your motives may be of the purest.—But I must remark that Nature takes no account of our motives, of our intentions, but of our ACTS *per se*. A doctor lately gave to two several women strychnine instead of some innocuous drug they asked for. He made a mistake : he did not intend to do any harm ;—but the women died. One of the saddest signs of our times is this deification of good intentions ; it leads directly to presumption—recklessness —for the blunderer (—his blunders made visible, *palpable*, by events,) points loftily to *the purity of his motives*, and in doing so is supposed to have done something to the purpose ! Uprightness of intentions *alone* does not bring back the dead, does not comfort the fatherless and widow in their affliction ; again, it does not restore confidence, revive trade—does not make contract a sacred thing and property secure. I have said so much on this point because you are a signal instance of a statesman whose activity has been, on the whole, purely mischievous—notwithstanding, nay, *in and through* his " good intentions " ! You are now, I have no doubt, elated (such your *goodness of intention !*) at the prospect of " settling " the Irish Question ; but be assured *you will fail.*[1]—And your good intentions will not save *others* from the *results* of your pernicious activity.

(iii) that I raise no question as to your intentions.

---

[1] A startling bit of self-portraiture is that contained in your letter addressed a few days ago to the Editor of the *Tuam Herald*—which, copied into a

Now in
showing that
you will fail,
I shall
consider—

I pass on now, after these indications of my spirit and my method, to the main considerations that I wish to lay before you. I proceed to support the statement I have made—that you will fail in your attempt to settle the Irish Question, to solve the Irish Problem, to remove the Irish Difficulty; and I will do so by examining your past record, your present position, and the leading qualities of your mind and character. And I will show that the present insoluble condition of the problem is due *exclusively* to your activity. I cannot hope, sir, to convince *you* of the soundness of my views; but, on the other hand, I cannot forget that I owe it to myself and to many men in the three kingdoms, not to let those who come after suppose that the moral Laws of the Universe, which you have in your previous activity consistently violated, were unknown —not yet ascertained—when you violated them; or that we are now helplessly looking forward to your declaration of policy on this Question as for words spoken by "the voice of a god and not of a man." I am not ambitious of posthumous fame: I address a very near posterity. I want the people who will live in this kingdom five, ten years hence to understand that your assumption of the *rôle* of Final Disposer of this Difficulty never deceived *us*—a few of your contemporaries,—that we know, not only that you must fail, but *why* you must fail. And it will be only fair to you, to them, to contemporary Englishmen and to ourselves, to explain *why*, in this matter, we are not, and cannot be, taken in. To this duty I now address myself; and I will from a multitude of topics make a selection of four or five for our special study. Our inquiry will thus be kept within reasonable bounds.

(1) the
essentia of
the
Difficulty:

I. First, then, I will state in the simplest formula I can construct, the *essentia* of the Difficulty, which manifestly you do not as yet rightly apprehend. Incidentally you will perceive the futility of all your measures, "generous" and other, to grapple with it. You have in fact been, *at best*, beating the air.

London paper, comes to my hand as I correct the proof of the above paragraph. You bring out clearly your "good intentions." Right! Lord Salisbury, being a man of infamous intentions, wouldn't solve the Irish Problem if he could.—Since writing this note, I find that somebody has been denying the authenticity of that letter. If it is not genuine, it is *ben trovato* [see p. 37]. We live in the days of *pilot balloons*.

II. I will glance at the *History* of the Difficulty down to the time when you made your first attempt to settle it. (ii.) the history of it ,

III. I will discuss your various attempts to settle the Difficulty ; and I will show that your early exertions rendered the solution of the Problem—before difficult, but every day becoming easier —prodigiously more difficult ; and that then—*at one blow*— you rendered solution impossible on this side Revolution. [Do you now, I may ask in passing, meditate Revolution? Are you prepared to stand in a white sheet for your past acts? I am sure you do not meditate Revolution ; and that you have (—such the determination of Destiny!) as yet found no place of repentance. Very well then : *you will fail.*] (iii.) your relation to it :

IV. As I desire not only to *criticize*, but to teach positive doctrine, I will describe the sort of statesman required at the present juncture : a man who, *properly supported*, could even now make the Irish Difficulty in a very short time " ancient history." And I will indicate in the most general terms his policy. You will thus have an opportunity of measuring the distance between you and a solution of this problem ; for, by how much you differ in mind, character, ways of thinking from the statesman hereinafter described, and by how much *your* policy will be found to differ from *his* policy,—by so much you will fall short of success in your present undertaking. (iv.) the statesman required to solve it ; and his solution.

I.

The *Essentia* of the Difficulty.

I will now explain the *essential* elements of the Irish Difficulty. In doing so, I beg you will understand that I know perfectly well what you and other people have by word or act asserted that the Difficulty consists in. But first, it will interest you as the statesman who has given so many days and nights to the study of this Difficulty, to be informed what the Difficulty—in essence— *is not*. The Difficulty in its essence lies—not in institutions,

The Difficulty, then, was not and is not connected with a Protestant Establishment, nor with Education of the primary, secondary, or university sort ; it has nothing to do with the land question, with landlords, land agents rack-rents, evictions, or

Dublin Castle. It does not exist because of "past misgovernment," pitch-caps, penal laws. It is not a result of the Union.
All these things have been and are mentioned by Irish orators—
whom I (in a sense) respect, and by their English dupes—for whom
I feel nothing but contempt—mentioned, I say, and emphasized—
one or other of them, from time to time. They are—some of them
pure *accidents*, others, only *symptoms* of the Difficulty. They are
not of the essence of the Difficulty; for if you could at this
moment blot out the reality and the remembrance of them, the
Difficulty in all its essentials would still remain. Well then, sir,
if this be so (and it *is* so)—you have been in this business as in
other things, fighting, wrestling, debating, retorting, scolding,
speechifying, rhetorizing—*in vain*,—you have been giving your
days and nights to what has been simply a series of costly, disastrous, bloody—*irrelevancies*. For you have addressed yourself
exclusively to *accidents*, to *symptoms :* you have never—never once
—touched, or even approached, the *essence* of the Difficulty.
All that you have ever done, all that you are doing now, all
that you will ever do, or can ever do—in the region you have
chosen for activity—amounts merely to solemn, wicked, and
pernicious *trifling !*

but in
character—
the character
of Celt and
Saxon ;
Now listen : The *essential* elements of the Irish Difficulty (which
means, I take it, the Difficulty that England has in ruling the
Irishry) lie in the fact, that between the typical Englishman and
the typical Irishman there exists a set of race-antagonisms almost
unparalleled in number and intensity. Observe, I do not say race-
antagonism. It is not that the Irish Celt hates the English Saxon
because the English Saxon is of a different race; but it is that if
you take the type-characters of the Celt, sift them, invoice them,
then do the like with the type-characters of the Saxon, and then
compare the two sets, you find *antagonism upon antagonism.* I
may say here that there exists a like series of antagonisms between
the Welsh Celt and the English Saxon ; and under your fostering
care the Welsh antagonisms will very soon be manifest. In the
general smash you will hear of the Welshman.

Now, many of the antagonisms which separate the Saxon from
the Celt (I confine my attention to the Irish Celt) do not concern

us at present. But some of them do ; let us look to those that do. They are of course those which bear on Society, Politics, Government. Now it happens that in this region the antagonism is rather more strongly marked than in any other ! The Celt (I speak now of the Saxon and Celt of *History*), left to himself, ever tends to relapse into barbarism, and when he gets there he stays there; in the Saxon there is a slight, but very slight, upward tendency towards civilization. The Celt tends to squat and breed and idle : the Saxon squats and breeds and moils—a foredoomed hewer of wood and drawer of water. The Celt has no idea of liberty ; "license" *he* "means when he cries liberty"; he is by nature turbulent, unruly, ungovernable—save by a strong, steady, consistent *external* pressure.[1] But when the *right man* comes along, the Celt is easily governed. The Saxon, on the other hand, as long as he can fill his belly, and in general be physically "comfortable," is very easily governed, and, left to himself, would even tend to evolve a rudimentary sort of government. The Celt is sensitive, sentimental, clever, "cute," ferocious,—an unscrupulous liar ; the Saxon is, by comparison, truthful,—"practical," *i.e.* material,— stupid, distrustful of mind, brutal. The Celt is a born fine gentleman ; the Saxon a born vulgarian. The Celt is, in a sense, logical— particularly, when the conclusion suits him ; he argues like an attorney : the Saxon, on the other hand, is almost wholly *below* reasoning ; and when he has evolved connected speech, explains that the world isn't governed by syllogisms. The Celt is, as regards religion, a superstitious devotee or an infidel ; the Saxon is a fanatic or a pagan.—Such, then, are the elements of the Difficulty.—But the Difficulty would never have come into existence if the two peoples had not been placed in direct contact—were they not connected at all, or connected only as subjects under a common empire. But let the Saxon be subordinated to the Celt, or the Celt to the Saxon : and lo, the Difficulty is born !

and yet, as I will now show, it was born of an accident.

[1] "Social order" is a plant not indigenous to Ireland.

II.

THE HISTORY OF THE DIFFICULTY.

The Saxon was pitchforked into mastership;

And now for a few remarks on the *History* of the Difficulty. The very form of words which I have just used implies that the subordination mentioned above has been effected. And the special form it took was—*that the Celt became subordinated to the Saxon.* Now please glance at the antagonisms I have noted in the previous section, and say whether it was possible in the nature of things that a " Difficulty " could be avoided. It is plain, in fact, that a Difficulty was inevitable. Let us see how it came about that the Saxon was pitchforked into the position of Master—a position for which his abilities nowise fitted him.

Towards the beginning of the eleventh century the polity that the Saxon, with everything in his favour, had been able to form—all that he was able to construct in the way of settled government, fell to pieces,—first and temporarily, under the repeated attacks of men of pure Scandinavian race,[1] secondly and permanently, under *one blow*—delivered by a Franco-Scandinavian people, the Normans.

---

[1] The Scandinavians (usually called *Danes*, but, in fact, *Norwegians*) were the first to introduce civilization into Ireland. What they did for the island may be gathered from a perusal of the third Section of Worsaae's great work : *Minder om de Danske og Nordmændene i England, Skotland og Irland: Kjöbenhavn,* 1851.—The men who leavened with true manliness the dwindling Saxon England of Æthelred "the resourceless" (*Unready*), who at the same time pushing on into the unknown North and planting their colonies in Iceland, thence passed on to Greenland,—thence to the continent of North America, establishing a settlement on the site of *New York* before Columbus was born or thought of—who introduced civilization into Ireland, and there had towns and churches and bishops of their own,—who wrested Neustria from the Frankish kings, and formed the *Varangian body-guard* of the Emperor at Constantinople—*these men,* I say, have not *as yet* had justice done them by the Muse of History. That same Muse of History, I may remark in passing, *if she inspires* certain writers of English and Irish history, is a lying baggage.— I quote from Worsaae a remarkable passage describing what the "Danes," did for civilization in Ireland. See Appendix, Note A.

The conquest by the Normans conferred on the Saxon the totally *irrelevant* gift of *Imperialism*—that is, of becoming the arbiter of the destinies of other peoples.　Before the Conquest, the Saxon knew Ireland only as the place to which he sold his children into slavery —Bristol being the head-quarters of the slave trade.[1]　Under one Norman king (Courtmantle) the Saxon became master of Ireland. Under another Norman king (Longshanks) Scotland and Wales were annexed.　From a Frenchman, *pur sang*, he received the dangerous boon of Parliamentary Government.—Thus Gurth the swineherd, the prototype of " Hodge " in powers and destiny, had " greatness thrust upon him " ; and thus the Difficulty was born. For the Norman element—the noblest that these islands have seen—began to dwindle,[2] partly through wars abroad and at home (the Hundred Years' War, and the Wars of the Roses) ; but principally through the sheer proletarian vigour of the Saxon. *Thus was Hastings avenged !* But thus, too, was the Saxon left to grapple with the *Difficulty* by his own unaided and absolutely inadequate powers.

How he succeeded let History tell.　His attempts to govern and, whilst Ireland, have been, in sum, simply one long-continued dotter-unfit for it ing ineptitude.　And now, to crown his ineptitude, he wants to sneak out of the responsibility—responsibility, which he has come to regard as the heaviest of burdens !　You see he had greatness *thrust upon him*.　He failed in the government of his rebellious dependency through sheer native incapacity.　He would for a long period be wholly unconcerned as to what went on in Ireland,—for had he not to tackle his less distant and more palatable cakes and ale ?　Then, when matters became intolerable even for him, he would rouse himself—meddle and muddle, try to mend, try to end,—or, perhaps, getting violent, he would hit out—and *of course* strike the wrong man.　Then the cold fit would come on again, and Disorder would have a free foot (as it has now) in Ireland.

---

[1] Some members of the family, *e.g.*, of Mr. John Morley (in the collateral branches) may, for anything I know, have been handed over *as slaves* to ancestors of Mr. Tim Healy in the direct line.—History repeats itself.

[2] It was never very large : there is never *very much* of the *best*—a fact which it behoves all French-Revolution Majority-mongers to bear in mind.

had his
difficulties
enormously
increased—

But the fumbling incapacity of the Saxon—his alternate fits of apathy and violence—did not constitute the ·whole of the evil. The stars in their courses fought against him.   By a strange fatality all that he valued in what he now calls his "progress" lessened his power of coping with the "Irish enemy,"—for so he had the sense to call the Celt in the fifteenth century.—I will mention three steps in his "progress" which have made—either the Difficulty greater, or his power to cope with it prodigiously less.

(i) by being
forced to
change his
religion;

1. In obedience to his Tudor master the Saxon became, in the sixteenth century, a "Protestant,"—but a Protestant in name only.   He is a born papist.   You are, *for the present,* ·his political pope.   "I cry *ditto* to Mr. Burke."—Thus the tension between the Celt (who did not become a Protestant, being in development not *up* to Protestantism, and being too sturdy to accept what he was not up to) and the Saxon (who had Protestantism thrust upon him through his native "flabbiness", and where *thinking* was required)—was enormously increased; insomuch that the ineradicable hatred of Irish Catholics to Protestantism has led even able observers into the mistake of supposing the Difficulty to have a religious and not a racial origin.[1]   There is no question that the difference of religion has enormously increased, though history shows that it did not originate, the Difficulty.   But in Catholicism as a religion there is nothing revolutionary—rather the reverse.   The Catholic Church has, as a rule, been on the side of order, property, civilization. And yet, in this case, racial hatred has actually, under our eyes, pressed the sanctions of religion into its service against the detested Saxon,—and the Catholic Church in Ireland is the tool of Irish-American Jacobinism !

(ii) by losing
his master—
the Nor-
man ;

2. During   many   centuries   the   noble,   manly,   independent,

[1] And then they go on—these able observers—to attribute the dislike of the Celt to Protestantism—to the "tyranny" of the Established Church !   I am not concerned to deny the "tyranny ;" there was very little, or rather none of it—but that is not the point :   the Celt does not object to tyranny, but he objects *to the Saxon*—and if the Saxon is a Protestant, then he hates Protestantism.—In later times presumptuous ignorance finds the Irish Establishment to be something that it—presumptuous ignorance—calls a *Upas tree.*—I have more to say on this very interesting vegetable—see pp. 66—71.

masterful Normans laboured to attain "constitutional freedom "—
a great blessing when a community feels the want of it, and fairly
wins and wears it. This the Norman community did. But, in
fairness, it shared the blessing with the Saxon, who *demanded* it
no more than our friend Hodge demanded *"this yer wote"* when
you "thrust" it upon him. Now, every step in the Saxon's
"constitutional progress" has been marked by an ever-increasing
inability to grapple with the Difficulty. For, as he would never
of himself have won the blessings of constitutional government,
—having had, in fact, in this case also, *greatness thrust upon him*,
—so he abused the gift. And he abused it in the two ways that
were natural—in his case, *inevitable* (1) Like the son of a rich
upstart, he was debilitated, debauched,—being put in possession of
advantages which he had not by his own exertions acquired ; and
a stern, consistent, manly course—such a course as would compel
the *respect* at least of his enemies—has become every day more
and more an impossibility. Our Saxon, having in our own
time obtained complete "constitutionalism,"—being master of the
situation, all enemies being put—*but not by himself*—under
his feet,—attains his maximum of incapacity to grapple with
the Irish Question ! Look at him ; he is absolutely unequal
to the discharge of the elementary functions of government
in Ireland ![1] He will not protect property, he will not enforce
contract, he will not evict, for an eviction is equal to "a sentence
of death" (you perceive he has learned some fine-sounding

---

[1] That there is no *necessary* connection between constitutional freedom and
"flabbiness" is proved by the noble struggle the Northern States of America
carried on for years against the states that wished to "repeal the Union." The
Southern States, whether they liked it or not, *were compelled by force to* STAY IN.
Right ! No fine talk here about "Southern ideas." This splendid persistency
of the Northern States is a spectacle that will cheer the real politician and the
friend of *true* progress as long as History is studied. And yet, I regret to say,
the struggle of the North against the South was sullied by the introduction of
the question of negro slavery. Government has nothing to do with such
"institutions." The North, in attempting to force "abolition" on the South,
was guilty of *tyranny*.—Very well : America has to face in the near future the
"Nigger Question", also—and for analogous reasons—the Socialist Question
and the *Irish* Question. The United States have more than one crisis ahead,
but their past action justifies the hope that they will get through all their
trials triumphantly.

phrases), he will not face the *fact*, that not to carry out an eviction means the break-up of civil society. And yet he *thinks* he is a statesman—and, perhaps, a saint—at any rate, *a friend of humanity ;* whereas he is, in matter of fact, a mere dottering coward, and a hypocrite to boot.—So much for the debility produced by privilege conferred on a creature who would, of and for himself, never have won it, nor cared to win it. (2) Again, the result of this saxon's being dowered with the priceless gift of constitutionalism is—that he, in sheer wantonness, dashes it to pieces ! And *that* introduces tyranny ; and *tyranny* is powerless to grapple with *any* " question." The English Constitution, thanks in a large measure to you, is in our time, to all intents and purposes, as obsolete as the Heptarchy. And when that *doctrinaire-littérateur*, your new Secretary for Ireland—the queerest fish, surely, that ever swam in such waters ![1]—jauntily told the House of Commons a few weeks ago that *he would exercise his discretion in consenting to the employment of Her Majesty's forces in carrying out evictions in Ireland*, that is, in determining whether the judgments of the Courts of Justice were to be carried out or set aside,—there was proclaimed, but not for the first time during your *régime*, the sad truth that the English Constitution is *dead*. In its place we have tyranny and anarchy ; and *they* never " settled " anything. Thus, sir, the development of the Constitution and its extinction have been equally unfavourable to the solution of the Irish problem.

(iii) by an outburst of lies abroad,   3. But I must notice one other historical event which has rendered prodigiously more difficult any settlement of this question. In the last decennium of the eighteenth century, a very remarkable event occurred in France. There was a sudden back-rush of society towards barbarism—an insurrection, namely, of the many against the few,—the many—filled, not with love of liberty (the idea is absurd !), but lust of material, sensual gratification. Through the abject cowardice of the few who *had* (and in this respect they were justly served) the many who *had not* were successful.—This insurrection of the *canaille* (they called themselves the *people*) is known in history as the FRENCH REVOLUTION. I have nothing

---

[1] If this were an appreciation of Mr. Morley as a literary man, I would give a very different account of him. But as a politician—!

further to do with it except to observe that it set in motion a fetid stream of *lies*, which has, in one or other of its ramifications, affected every community in Europe, and no community more banefully than our own. We expended some £400,000,000 in the struggle with the lies (in concrete form, of course) flung abroad in that upheaval of *the worst.* And yet we are now, as a nation, the slaves, either of the original lies, or of others, their direct offspring. Should you like to know what I mean by these lies? I will make a list of a few, which have a particular bearing on the Irish question. I have only to *remind* you of some of them ; you have heard them before :—

which lies he fought against, but now professes to believe— shaping them into such form as—

1. Force is no remedy.
2. Ireland must be governed by Irish ideas.
3. Is not he (a certain person) a man and a brother ?
4. Is he (a certain person) not our own flesh and blood ?
5. An eviction is equivalent to a sentence of death.
6. Property has its duties as well as its rights.[1]
7. Every man born in a country has a right to be able to live in that country ; and one man has as good a right to live as another.
8. The soil of a country belongs to the *people* (*i.e., the canaille*) of that country.
9. The state is bound to provide labour (or rather the product of capital and labour, *i.e. wealth*) for *certain* citizens.
10. Violence and crime are evidences of *political discontent*, (—*not* of *social rottenness*,) and their remedy is—" *concession.*"
11. All members of the upper classes are devils incarnate ; all members of the lower classes are suffering angels.
12. One nation governs another solely for the benefit of *the people* of that other.

Now, sir, these statements (for the *questions* [3 and 4] are only *rhetorical* questions—questions equivalent, that is, to strong affirmative statements—) are either mainly or wholly *lies.* When I say *lies*, I speak of the statements in themselves ; I am not thinking of those who make, repeat or love them.[2] By whomsoever

---

[1] This is usually cited by those who are preparing to pounce on other people's property.

[2] I desire to insist on this. But I cannot use any other word than the ugly

made, repeated, or loved they are flagrant violations of the *truth*
of things—of the *facts* of the Universe. Some are pure, downright, stark-naked *lies.* Some contain the half-truth which, as a
vehicle, carries down the *lie*—hidden, unperceived, unsuspected—
with all its pernicious consequences. I will spend a few words
in explanation of this statement. I will analyse two or three of
these propositions, and will bring to light the lurking, specious,
hypocritical LIE " held in solution " in each.

Take proposition 2. It concerns Ireland.

(a) "Ireland must be governed by Irish ideas;"

" Ireland must be governed by Irish ideas."

Now, by whomsoever made, were it " Hilarion or holy Paul," this
proposition contains, first and foremost, an ambiguity. " Ireland "
—that is clear; " Irish "—*there* comes in the ambiguity. What
did the framer of this proposition mean by " *Irish*" ? There are
two WHOLLY ANTAGONISTIC communities that call themselves Irish.
The Ulsterman, and the capitalist everywhere, do *still*, and the
landed gentry all over Ireland *did*—up to the epoch of your
" healing measures," which beggared and banished them,—call
themselves *Irish.* But also, the bitterest enemies of the British
Empire and the English race, and of the " Irish " classes just
mentioned, called themselves then, and call themselves now, *Irish.*

Which class, I wonder, was before the intellectual consciousness
of the man who framed this famous proposition ? I cannot tell ;
I only know that I have heard it again and again quoted by the
men whom I have in this paper called *the Irishry*, the men who
hate England first and the devil afterwards—quoted as a *justifi-*

one—*lie*, because the statements above have exactly the effect on society
which *deliberate violations of the truth* would have. It is better in public
affairs *to do the right thing* with a wrong motive—than to do the wrong thing
with the best of motives. *Nature* looks to our acts, not to our motives. *Religion*
considers *both*. And *here* we are face to face with *Nature*,— and break her laws
at our peril! *Nature* doesn't care a bawbee whether we are "steeped to the
lips " in piety, or are as impious as the " Hermokopids." If we fling ourselves
over Beechy Head, we shall not be saved from instant destruction though the
odour of our sanctity should assail the nostrils of the crew and passengers of
the German Lloyd's steamer *Habsburg*—or other suitable vessel—passing up
Channel at the time. And if we keep *well in* from the edge of the cliff, we
may believe—and *there* maintain (with Gibbon)—that " all forms of religion are
—to the peasant equally true, to the philosopher equally false, and to the
magistrate equally useful " !

cation of their relentless hostility to England. Now, which of these populations are indicated in the adjective *Irish* here? Did the speaker mean the *Irishry*—or the *English and Scotch in Ireland?* The phrase is hopelessly ambiguous.

Well, but having ascertained by our own knowledge all that *could* have been in the mind of the framer of this proposition, we next proceed to examine the statement in the light of *truth* —of *facts*.

1. Suppose the framer of it (he was a great "speaker") didn't know, or didn't *realise* the truth in regard to the two different and conflicting populations in Ireland : in that case there is of course nothing further to be said—except, indeed, that he uttered words of most mischievous consequence.

2. But suppose he knew Ireland as *we* know it. The phrase is still open to serious objection :—

(*a*) Did he mean by *Irish* in the phrase—"Irish ideas"—the Ulsterman, or, in general, the England-loving, England-representing, Protestant element in Ireland? If he did—*which is not likely*—I object to the phrase unless with most vital qualification. I object to any "ascendency" in Ireland or anywhere else, other than ascendency such as strict conformity to the laws of Nature confers. Let an industrious, sober, thrifty man live ; let an idle, good-for-nothing, thriftless creature get out of the way as soon as he can !¹ That's the true doctrine. But—pardon me—I object to "ascendency" derived from accident of race or religion. That a man is a Protestant, is, in so far as the State is concerned, —*nothing ;* that he loves or hates England is nothing ; but that he pays his way ; that he is obedient to the laws of society ; that he owes no man anything ; all this is very much. But all this is, or was, fulfilled by many men who write their names with a *Mac* or an *O*, and go to "chapel" on the Sunday.—I object to Ulster ascendency, or *any* ascendency, that is not based on the punctual, honourable payment of debts, the stern, stringent discharge of all obligations that have been *voluntarily* undertaken. Honest men—and no other—of whatever race or religion, make

¹ And, *in fact*, the industrious and sober *will live*, and the idle and drunken *will die*, whether you like it or not. All things will *in the end* be well.—But what an amount of needless misery is caused *in the meantime !*

C

a nation truly great. And, let me tell you, these qualities will ultimately give the individual or the community that possesses them
" ascendency," though all the brute force in the world should be
thrown into the scale against them.

(*b*) Again, did the speaker mean by " Irish ideas" the ideas
of the Irishry ? If so, it was a most astounding utterance. The
only distinct idea of the Irishry—the idea, that is, on which all are
at one—is the idea—of turning the English out of Ireland. Well,
Englishmen may be so " liberal," so " generous," as to look with
equanimity on their being kicked out of Ireland (especially when
the kicking is suffered vicariously by " their own flesh and blood "
—by men who in sentiment are more English than the English) ;
but if they do, their liberality—their generosity—mean, in truth,
only staggering senility—the immediate precursor of dissolution,
the herald of the tomb.

No, Sir : the true doctrine is (—unfortunately there is no public
man in England courageous enough to proclaim it ; if there were,
he would say)—*Ireland is part of an Empire which our forefathers
built up. We mean to preserve that Empire intact, not only from
a feeling of duty, but from the stronger pressure of the feeling of
self-interest. Life is a* struggle *for nations as for individuals ;
and we* must *fight* our corner. *Ireland with its four millions
shall be governed by the " ideas" that make for the welfare of
some three hundred millions of the human race, for whom we
are responsible—and are proud to be responsible. And the position
of Ireland —so near the heart of the Empire, and therefore, by
possibility, so dangerous, shall be taken into account in our every
act, in our every utterance ; and if Ireland contains four million
rebels—supported by the dollars of as many as " seventeen nationalities" on the other side of the Atlantic, those four million rebels, and
those " seventeen nationalities" must be made to feel that they have
met their match.*[1]—Ireland to be governed by Irish (*i.e.* rebel) ideas !
Yet, I fear the statesman who uttered these words meant, in a
hazy way of course, *the ideas of the Irishry.* At any rate, the pernicious doctrine involved has been, to some extent, followed (to

---

[1] For the conclusions of sound statesmanship on the Irish Question, see
Section IV.

some extent, as compared with what it will be in the near future)
—and the result ?—Why, that, at this moment, not only Ireland,
but *the whole Empire* is *governed by Irish ideas!*—So much on
this famous proposition,—which involves, first, an absurd ambiguity,
—then, translated into act, either an injustice—a *real* injustice—
to Ireland, or an act of treason against the English people.

I promised to deal with two of the lies. I will now take the
second lie, but I must despatch it in few words—*"Is he not a
man and a brother?"* The question (let us suppose) is, whether
we shall confer a certain privilege (say the suffrage : but *that* is now
called a *right!*) on a certain person who is, by many, held to be
not qualified to receive it. Against this conviction of many persons,
and by way of annihilating it, a certain Jacobin orator projects the
query (as the *Polyphemus* might project a torpedo)—*" Is he not a
man and a brother?"* That is, he, *of course,* is "a man and a
brother."—Now, let us examine this proposition. *" He is a man."*
True : I never questioned his sex. And I never supposed him to
be an oyster, or even a gorilla. He is a man—*vir* and *homo.* *"A
brother."* That depends. As a matter of *fact,* the man in question
is not, and could not be, the son of my (personal) father and
mother. But he that is an orator must show himself oratorical ;
and what the orator here means is—that the person in question
ought to be treated *as if he were* a brother, with Christian kindliness, &c., &c. Now, I am quite ready to treat him with Christian
kindliness and charity. I am quite willing, as far as possible, to
satisfy the high standard of ἀγάπη set forth in that famous
scripture, 1 Cor. xiii. But am I in Christian charity bound to make
this man *arbiter of my destiny ?—Not so.* There is not a word in
1 Cor. xiii. recommending such a course. I meet the orator
fairly. I *do* treat this man as a brother. The orator asks me
to do so, and I have done so. But *give him the suffrage?* That
is quite another matter. The conviction that he *is* "a man and
a brother" may lead me, in pure charity,—not to say, in mere self-
defence—to *deny* him a privilege which his ignorance would in all
probability lead him to abuse.[1] But again, if this man is *my*

(b) " Is he
not a man
and a
brother?":

---

[1] I am here arguing as if I granted postulates which I by no means grant.
Of course, the right doctrine is, that no man has a claim to the franchise who

brother, surely I am *his* brother? And surely *he* ought, in *his*
treatment *of me*, to follow 1 Cor. xiii.? Brotherhood is all very
well,—but, for my part, I don't *see* the brotherhood—in any sense
—of the man who smashes my shop-windows, or who in public
proclaims or applauds the desire to hang me on the nearest lamp-
post, because (as it happens) I have been very self-denying, in
order (let us say) that I may support an invalid "brother"—not
of the oratorical, but of the actual " flesh-and-blood " sort. And
—as to placing my destiny in the hands of such "brothers"—
though it has been done, I would as soon think of selecting a tiger
to be my guide through a jungle.

(c) "Force is
no remedy."   So much in regard to the two leading lies in the list which I
have made out.—But the politics of the hour compel me to notice
one other lie in the list—a third lie—because it confronts us just
now in every " Liberal " newspaper we take up. The lie I refer to
is the lie I have indicated in the formula—" *Force is no remedy*."
One word on this lie. The form it takes at present in regard to
Ireland is :—" *We cannot return to the odious practice of Coercion*."
And you will be fortunate if you are not informed how many " Coercion " measures have been introduced since the Union—the in-
ference, expressed or understood, being that the Union was a
mistake, and that " Coercion " has been a failure. Now, leaving
the Union out of account, let us examine the meaning of this cry
against Coercion. Let us in the first place look at *facts.*—I lived
in Ireland during that reign of terror—the reign of Coercion.
Well, the sun was not darkened nor the moon turned to blood ; in
short, I didn't know—otherwise than through the newspapers—
that Coercion, that odious thing which England "cannot again
resort to," existed ! But, on second thoughts, *why should I*—how
could I—perceive its existence? *Your own* measure of Coercion
(passed when, apparently, you fell into panic terror the moment the

does not by his own unaided exertions *win* it. For, look you, it is not a *right*
but a *privilege*—else why not give it to everybody—to all the men, women,—
and *curates*, as Sydney Smith would add,—in England? And nothing is more
fatal to manliness in an individual or a state than a privilege won by *this*
man, and by him conferred on *that*. Finally, the man who fairly wins for
himself a privilege is the man who will worthily wear it. Of course, therefore,
the main question is, not whether this man will *abuse* the privilege, but whether
he *can win* it.

murderer's knife cut *high-official* throats—a result you owe, believe me, to the fumbling incompetence of your government,—to your months of previous trifling with murders at least a score—to selfish profligacy—or to all three)—your own pet measure of coercion, I insist, and *I know what I am talking about*—troubled no Irishman who was not either a criminal, a rebel, or (as was very frequently the case) *both*. As I was *neither*, I never knocked my nose against your "Coercion."

But now, coming to the general question : *Is* force no remedy ? If it be no remedy, why have you ever engaged in war—I beg pardon, in military operations ? Why did an English admiral commit what, if force is no remedy, was the *senseless crime* of bombarding Alexandria ? What is the meaning of the "operations" by which thousands of brave Arabs, "rightly struggling to be free," were mercilessly shot down by men who (not being superior persons, but simply frank Englishmen of the best type) were disgusted—soldiers by profession though they were—and rendered all but mutinous by the repulsive duty which you thrust upon them as troops of the Queen ? You, I presume, saw that Force here *was* a remedy—though I didn't. If force is no remedy, then open to-morrow all the prison doors in England. And in respect of "Coercion," lay your hand on your heart, and say— have you abandoned it ?—abandoned it at home, abandoned it abroad ? *If you have*, your public activity *must*, in the very nature of things, tend to bring about the Decline and Fall of the British Empire.[1] No community, since the world began, ever existed—much less attained or preserved ascendency over other nations—under such conditions.

[1] I must not be supposed to argue that Coercion—indeed, that exceptional legislation in any shape or form has been necessary—in the nature of things— during the thirty-odd years that I have known Ireland. The very reverse is the case. The institutions which our unenlightened forefathers left us were amply sufficient "to carry on the Queen's Government," had our "statesmen" (what a ludicrous misnomer !) been men of the right sort. *They*, in fact, have been themselves the living *necessity* for Coercion ; and, therefore, are no more justified in applying it than would be a foolish father who should thrash his son for being sick from an over-dose of sweetmeats, which sweetmeats the father forced him to eat !—I can well understand the Irishman's hatred of Coercion. As applied by the saxon "Government" he can see no *sense* in it. He knows that he is always *consistently disloyal*. Why this inconsistency in punishment ?

But really, events are moving so fast, this drama of dissolution
is developing its catastrophe with such startling rapidity, that I find
on writing a paragraph on what is at the time debatable matter,
that the actual state of affairs about us sets aside all my argument
by proving it up to the hilt—by giving all the corroboration that I
could reasonably expect in ten years.   I have been denying the
statement that " force is no remedy," and I have been asserting
that force *is* a remedy—and the *only* remedy in many cases.   And
I assert that it is, in the present case, the sole and only remedy.
Now up comes this week's number of that very able journal,
United Ireland.   And remember, *United Ireland* always *means*
what it says :—

"One portion of their programme the Irish people could realise at once.
Before another winter was over landlords would be paupers.   The rest would
come in the vicissitudes that are ever lowering over a great flabby empire, with
an overgrown population, decaying trade, and millions of deadly enemies in its
bosom.[1]   The most stupendous parliamentary scandal ever witnessed would be
followed by the most horrible suppressed civil war beheld in a country where
every peasant has learnt to laugh at the terrors of the gaol and the plank-bed, and
to treat his rulers to all the inconveniences of armed insurrection without handling
a gun.   And all the while Liberal progress in England would be at a stand-
still, and the Liberal party split into fractions : one part watching the terrorisation
of Ireland in an agony of helpless shame ; and the other dragged at the chariot-
wheels of a Brummagem Cromwell."

Now, what do you think of that ?   Ireland can conduct a
rebellion "without handling a gun."   Exactly: but since the
world began no human being could conduct a rebellion *without*
" handling a gun "—*or what stood for a gun.*   What a commentary
on the completeness—absoluteness, of the surrender which you
have made to the Irish party !   Suppose you had the duty laid
upon you of making the Ireland—so graphically described—once
more a part of the Queen's dominions, *what would you do ?*
Observe, *United Ireland*, always frank, speaks of the "inconveniences of armed insurrection"—*that is force.*   How are you
going to meet it ?—But in truth the statement is a sheer *hypocrisy ;*
and that is the reason why *United Ireland* is so jubilant.   Force *is*
a remedy ; and the man who says it is not will be found the next
minute *using it as a remedy.*[2]

[1] *Quite true!* This writer knows what he is talking about.

[2] But *force* must be distinguished from (what England usually employs)
uncertain, senseless, inconsistent, irritating, exasperating *violence*.

In closing this section I must make a few remarks on *the saxon* Look at him now— *in Modern England*, and I ask your particular attention to them. Don't lose time carping at my ethnological theories ; let Professor Freeman, if he is so minded, do that. I don't care a straw whether, for example, the characteristics I am about to describe go with saxon blood or not.[1] Rather I am concerned that they are *here*—here in the England that we have to live and work in— here in force, here a menace and a danger *because by you made supreme.* The greasy, hypocritical philanthropism of the time has done much to breed, to nurse, and to perpetuate them ; but *you* have made them *supreme in the state.* Understand, then, that although I speak of the saxon in concrete form, I have my eye rather on well-marked *tendencies*—a clearly manifested *spirit—in us as a people.* The saxon, then, is still among us. Behold him !

Inept, resourceless, brutal, self-indulgent, selfish, cowardly, cruel, on the lower levels of society ; —the grand cause, I insist, of weakness and danger to this com- munity,—you have him in all ranks ; you meet him at every turn ; but the lower you go, you find him in ever-increasing numbers. He it is who *'eaves 'arf a brick* at a "stranger." He comes to your hall-door when you are absent, and won't go away till he is paid for so doing ; the brute takes the chance that you are not present to give him a kicking ;—or perhaps he believes you hold the (to him) comfortable doctrine that "force is no remedy." If, in the guise of a "working man," he comes to your house and gets a job, he has not the ability—or the will—to do good work : he has just cunning enough to make two days' work out of one, and leave something to do at another time. Then, if he can get "no work to do" (—a lie in nine cases out of ten ; if he exerted himself to get employment as he exerts himself to tell all the world he can't get it,—and if he kept it when he got it,—he would seldom be idle), he marches in procession about the suburbs of London levying black- mail on the silly (saxon) inhabitants. Or he goes (*with his pipe in*

---

[1] In fact, I want an epithet. Will my non-saxon readers suggest one ? If they are non-saxon, they know what I *mean* by *saxon.* What I mean by "saxon" is *almost* what Mr. Matthew Arnold means by *Philistine*—not quite, however ; for I find he lately addressed, at some church blow-out in the East End, remarks (and sad stuff they were) to an audience which *I* should have pronounced saxon to the core, but which he, clearly, would not have

his mouth)[1] to the Mansion House (where a lot of "philanthropical" busybodies are just now distributing to knaves and blackguards the contributions of cowards and of fools), and having received, as *his* share of the "ransom," the sum of three shillings, he rushes off to his mates, transported with indignation, and damns the eyes of "*this yer bloomin' Mansion 'Ouse Fund,—only three bloody bob, and beef at elevenpence a pound ! Blowed if the working man ought to stand it !* "—A truly *imperial* creature, you perceive ! Who could have the face to deny the franchise to such a man and a brother ?—He expects to be tipped if you bid him good-day. At the ports (Liverpool, Sunderland, &c.) he—calling himself a British sailor— raises an agitation against the employment of foreign sailors by British shipowners, though foreign sailors are cheaper, steadier, more obedient and orderly—in short, more efficient and valuable —than he. And in the East End of London he just now desires mightily that a *Judenhetze* could be got up against foreign Jews who, coming to London, are glad to do the work he refuses to do —who are thrifty, industrious, temperate ; and who, as he complains in one of the newspapers, beginning on nothing, soon contrive to possess and occupy the best houses in the street ! What free-born Englishman could stand that ?[2]

—on the higher levels :   Placed in a higher social position he goes to school to play football, and (a vulgarian in the grain) *to get into a nice set ;* and his idea of university life is—moiling at books for an academic bribe, or training for a boat race. His "sport" usually involves

pronounced *Philistine.* By the way, considering the *matter* of that speech, I am constrained to pronounce him (Mr. Arnold !) to be a very Goliath of Gath, —on each hand six fingers and on each foot six toes—four-and-twenty in number —and the staff of his spear like a weaver's beam !

[1] You and I never get tobacco *for nothing.*

[2] For him, idlers of his own type but in the "higher" ranks, get up societies, associations, tea-parties, what not—with the object of making his life *bright* —of making his surroundings "*a little less unlovely* "—of relieving "the dreadful monotony of toil." True ! toil grudgingly given—given as our saxon gives it— is to him, thank Heaven, *a dreadful monotony.* But the relief he wants is not such as a parcel of *dilettanti* patrons are willing to afford. The *pub.* is more to his "mind." Even the Church (God help us !) is making her services "shorter and brighter" for the special benefit of our saxon. For him, too, the *sansculotte*-saxon State invades the rights of property in order that he may be comfortably "housed."

the *death* of the so-called-"lower" animals. Entrusted with
public duties, he, in sheer stupidity, or from low, profligate,
murderous *greed*, furnishes our army in the field with rifles
that jam, bayonets that bend like nail-rod, tinned meat that is
rotten, and hay containing a tidy make-weight of brickbats.
Promoted to having a hand in public *policy*, he sends out an
immense quantity of railway plant to a certain port on the Red Sea,
and "in the interests of civilization" (for at this stage he is *articulate*,
and is, moreover, inoculated with the virus of French Revolutionism) he begins to lay down a railway from this obscure Red
Sea port to—nowhere in particular. Then he is seized with panic,
and fear of what he calls "blood-guiltiness," and thinks he will
leave the railway to be worked by the Arabs. It will tend, don't
you see? to civilize them.[1] But unfortunately the Arabs don't
"see" it, nay, they have the bad taste (or good sense) to *burn*
the railway line punctually as it is made from day to day ! Then,
as all the world knows that railway plant is like a consumptive,
and benefits by a sea voyage, he gives all the railway plant left by
the Arabs *another* fortnight at sea on the way back to England,
and finally deposits it in Woolwich marshes.[2]

He it is who (being, of course, utterly ignorant of history) wants
to know what the House of Lords ever did for the *people* (meaning
the *canaille*)?[3] And every time that assembly shakes itself free
from the influence of saxon proletarianism, and gives a straight,

---

[1] A cargo of moral pockethandkerchiefs will operate powerfully in the same
direction.

[2] And talking of Woolwich—he (a true saxon, but one of the baser-official
sort) has to load a steamer, bound for Egypt, with military stores of various
kinds. Well, he is careful (this is a *fact*) to stow away all the *light* material as
near to the keel as possible, and the heavy ammunition (a thing that a man
likes to have handy, of course : one can't tell the minute one will require a live
shell)—high up towards the hurricane deck. However, the captain (happen-
ing not to be in my sense of the word, a saxon) refused to go to sea till
the centre of gravity got a little nearer the keel and a little farther from the
main yard ; and so the vessel *didn't* founder in the Bay. I can't tell what the
whole transaction *cost*.

By the way—How about the cargoeing of the steamer *Elephant* which some
time ago left the Thames, having on board the machinery of the *Impérieuse*
(building, I think, at Plymouth), and *was never heard of?*

[3] To which I would reply : *The less the better.*

manly vote, he raises the cry:—"*Down with the House of Lords !*"—But his peculiar delight is to speak insultingly of the Royal Family—even of the August Lady who so worthily occupies (and long may she occupy!) the throne of Monmouth, Longshanks, Court-mantle, and (a greater than any one of the three) Guilielmus Conquestor. He will even (—when pitchforked into the position of *legislator* by the same mysterious—and, in this case, *most* mysterious—Providence that has at the present juncture placed *you* in the position of chief Minister of the Crown,[1] and committed to *you* the destinies of England), he will, I say, be guilty of the brutal and senseless, the merely *disgusting* (but truly "saxon") social crime of keeping his seat and *hissing* when the health of his Sovereign is proposed. This *bêtise* is *his* way of showing that he is an independent, downright Englishman : no dam-nonsense about *him*, you know. And his pals in office are suddenly struck blind and deaf,—as well they might be, at so scandalous, so abominable, a spectacle.[2] Again, he trips up your Government, by refusing to pass a vote of money to maintain the Royal Parks—a vote as routine in its character as any possible vote of money towards upholstering the seats in the House of Commons. But the word *Royal* he couldn't stand.—Now it is a muddle in the Admiralty accounts ; now it is a scandal at the War Office ; now it is abuses in the Civil Service ; now it is the condition of Scotland Yard ; anon it is the condition of the Navy. If he is not meddling *here*, it is because he is muddling *there*. If he is not plundering in Ireland, it is because he is blundering in Egypt. And occasionally, when the fit is on him, he meddles and muddles, plunders and blunders, in the same place and at the same time ! But woe to the man who is nearest to John Bull's horn when he rouses himself and "goes for" *somebody*—it may occasionally happen that he goes for the guilty party ; but his attack is due merely to the fact that he is *irritated*. He does not try to find

[1] On second thoughts—there is no mystery about it. Mr. Parnell is the Providence, and, to do him justice, there is (save in his occasional disappearances) nothing mysterious about him. His *policy* is as clear as the day, though you don't see it.—But perhaps you do ?

[2] By the way, I never heard that Charles Russell was thought either blind or deaf by poor clever John Rea in the old Belfast days. Of course, "many things have happened" since then.

the *causes* of his irritation. In short, he has a *go* at something, and then—the hot fit over—he will sink into slumber, and abuses will have "a high old time" once more. But whatever he does or fails to do, the trail of the *saxon* is over it all.

I have already indicated *your* relation to the saxon. You, sir, HAVE MADE HIM SUPREME in the kingdom, and with fatal results to the kingdom—and to *him*. He is to be found in the highest class; but he *swarms* in the lowest class. And you have made the lower (or lowest) class supreme. It is *"par excellence" the* class of the saxon. You have, therefore, achieved his apotheosis. He is now a god, and you are his prophet, his *Flamen Dialis.* And in this point of view you are to me a very pathetic figure. With a look on your face of ascetic, devotional, reproving gravity (so admirably depicted by John Tenniel in his immortal *Punch* cartoon of "The Augurs") you stand before the idol you have set up—a monster with many hands, many heads, no brains; its most *prominent* feature, the stomach!—And you "Cry aloud, for it is a god!" Now, sir, you have made this thing the ruler of the destinies of the British Empire. And yet, its godship does little but produce creatures—(in this sense it is, indeed, a *creator*)—mouths that must be filled, backs that must be clothed, not by the providence of this god (providence not being among the number of its divine attributes), but by *me* and people like me. *We* find the money; *this thing* spends it. That is your arrangement.—

But wait a while. That I shall be taxed to the point at which taxation becomes intolerable; that I shall feed and "educate" people with whom I have no connection,—whom I have never seen, and for whom I have no more responsibility than I have for the existence of any individual rabbit in any conceivable rabbit-warren on the surface of the planet—that I shall be called upon, nay, forced by all the "resources of civilization" at the disposal of a brutal government (truly saxon) to undertake these *factitious* duties,—in plain English to submit to these nefarious impositions, —while if I am an Irish subject *of a certain class*, the same organization will *decline* to discharge the *real* duties—even the most elementary—of all government in regard to me: I say this sort of thing may flourish *for a time*, but it hastens to its end.

again—as your god:

and—as a multiplying parasite.

Wait till your saxon god—your *Jupiter Sator*—has exercised his darling, his peculiar, his characteristic god-function up to a certain point, and the tension on me and my like will come *not* to the " *sticking* " but the *breaking* place.   In short, I shall be unable to support those that are (as if it were *of right*) quartered upon me. I sink, and nobody cares about me.   I have been a " selfish " landlord or a " grinding " capitalist : but what becomes of those whom my exertions find in food, clothing, and " education " ? What becomes of the (so-called) " working man " who makes me work for him—who does not work for me, but yet claims—and receives—wages (at least *money*) which I must furnish ?   In other words, what becomes of the parasite when the organism on which it feeds ceases to live ?   A flea or bug may live merrily, enjoy life hugely,—think it in fact *decidedly* " worth living " when it lives ·on me or on you—*as long as we too are alive.*   The bug, the flea, must have blood—a commodity we can't supply for ever ; we may desire to do so, it is true,—especially as a high authority assures us that they (the bug and flea) are " our own flesh and blood "— *as they are* only too truly !   When we can't feed our parasites any longer, please say what becomes of—the parasites ?

What is to become of—*him ;*   When (—flea and bug aside—and I wish they were very much aside) I cease to be able to pay my share of the imperial and local taxes, what becomes of the children of other people, whom I, by legislative mandate, and no thanks to me, feed, clothe, and " educate " ?   But once more : what if I, foreseeing the *inevitable* transition from the state of *tension* to the state of *breaking*,—measuring accurately all that is foreshadowed by the declamations of the gentry who talk of *ransom*, &c., remove myself and all the property that is left me—to another hemisphere ?   What will become of the ruler of our destinies, the " working man " ?—I will tell you what will become of him : he will be brought face to face with *Famine ;* and if at the same time he have *War* forced upon him, he and those about him will see a state of things such as I, for my part, don't care to contemplate.   God forbid that we should come to this pass ; but mark me, we are, as a people, doing all we can to bring about the state of things I have sketched.   Put in a nutshell, the question is simply this : What will you do when the wealth-finder (the sources of his wealth drying up day by day) ceases, of necessity, to be able to bear the *ever-increasing* horde that live upon him?—And coming back to our argument, how can you expect that a people in the economical condition I have just described will ever "settle" any political or social question whatever? The sole problem with them will soon be—*to get enough to eat.* Yet they—these starving *prolétaires*—elect our legislators, and occupy exclusively the legislative activity of our "legislators" when these are elected. But again (I will presently return to this consideration), suppose we didn't get to the point of actual starvation, do you really imagine that the sort of person I have described above—the sort of person *you have made supreme*—will help you to settle the Irish, or any other question? Never believe it. He has neither the mental nor the moral power that would fit him to help you. You have gone down to the gutter for your supporters; and there are those who say (*I* don't) that you went to the gutter because you knew that there alone you *would get* supporters. You have smashed the Constitution in order to double a constituency which before was, God knows, many times too large.[1]

Well, you got your "capable citizens"; and now with what result? Why, that you thereby *made the Irish Question insoluble.* — the Irish Question; Nemesis, you see, has followed pretty swiftly. You have a House of Commons (I don't now refer to the Irish party) so ludicrously incapable of any sound and manly legislative work that—we need say no more about it.[2] The legislative instrument at your disposal, could you even now bring forward anything to the purpose on this Irish Question, would be unequal to the task of giving it a fair and full discussion. Yet you have had the making

---

[1] The desire of every Englishman who loves his country ought to be an all-round *disfranchising* statute. That is what Edmund Burke, the *Quinbus Flestrin* of English statesmen, so ardently desired. And I cry—"Ditto to Mr. Burke!" But such a statute—since the French Revolution, and till we come to the crash that will mend us or end us, has been and will be impossible. Truth is truth, however, all the same.—There is only one all-round disfranchising statute, that I know of, in English History (8 Hen. VI. c. 7, A.D. 1430). What a lesson for legislators!

[2] In fact, political questions have as good as ceased to be referred to in the House of Commons, which is becoming a sort of Social Science (or rather Social Ignorance) Congress. It discussed the other day a Crofters' Bill—which will of course be as mischievous in result as the Irish Land Bill of 1881. [See

of that instrument ! And just destiny drives you to apply an instrument, artificially weakened by yourself (and, some would say, in your own interest), to a bit of work which, at its strongest, it failed to do !

—and the Empire?

Lastly, under this head, I ask : Is the term *saxon* interchangeable with *Englishman ?* God forbid ! If so, we are indeed undone. But I believe there are still in England thousands of men of all ranks, creeds, and parties, who exhibit none of the characteristics I have ascribed to the "saxon." Upon these upright, honest, thrifty, clear-sighted, patriotic men the fate of the Empire will *ultimately* depend. By such men it was built up, to whatever stock they belonged, and by such, and such alone, can it be preserved. But it must first go into the fire of Revolution, and it *may* never come out again.[1] Unfortunately, *political* power (which in a healthy state would always lie alongside *moral* power) has been cut adrift, and now rests, not with the best, but with those who must *necessarily* be the worst. Our body politic, grievous sick,—tottering under the ever-hardening and ever-spreading leprosy of Socialism,—is summoned to confront what would have taxed all the energies it possessed in its best days.— The Irish Question, sir, will not be solved by *you.* But there is no intrinsic insolubility in it. The " Difficulty " is, in truth, solely and absolutely on *this* side of the Irish Sea. England, engaged in strangling what are the *best* elements within her own borders—the

Appendix, Note B.] Loud cries of dissent greeted Mr. Goschen's* truism (but truisms must now be stated as if they were paradoxes) that the right of free sale "meant a higher rent to the next tenant." And one Mr. Barclay retorted that the choice was between free sale and rack-rents ! I don't suppose it ever occurred to this Mr. Barclay to inquire whether there is or could be such a thing as a *rack*-rent.

[1] But let us be just. That England must (and she *certainly* must, or all history is a lie) go through " cleansing fires "—in which she may be consumed— is due to the fact that the good elements in her were dormant—when they ought to have been alive and active. And *in so far as they were dormant*, they, of course, were not good, but bad elements.

---

* Mr. Goschen—a most singular and ever perplexing phenomenon ! A man with (apparently) eyes to see, but without the heart to dare—a man who reaches out towards, and all but touches, yet is destined never to touch—greatness ! I wouldn't, for a good deal, stand in his shoes. His will be the sentence pronounced on the Church at Laodicea.

elements which alone could "settle" the Irish Question—is not
very likely to settle the question by the aid of the *worst* elements,
however triumphant these may be ; however loud their brayings on
grasping (*Te duce, Cæsar !*) the helm of the state.

I have now described the " saxon " element—the element (call
it by whatever name you please) that makes for our destruction ;
and I have shown that you have given it such prominence and
influence—(principally by your *recent* legislation, though your
Ballot Act favoured it powerfully),[1] that it is now supreme in Parliament.   I have shown—and I don't think you could successfully
traverse my assertion—that this element is powerless to grapple
with *any* great question, and least of all with a question bristling
with difficulties like the Irish Question.   The present Parliament,
and any Parliament elected on your own special Gladstonian
franchise, can only cry " Ditto to Mr. Gladstone," or—turn you
out.[2]   Debate, discussion, is obsolete.   Suppose, then, you should
bring in a *really healthy measure*, you couldn't be certain (and
this you have brought upon yourself) that the House would
appreciate it, and follow you and pass your Bill.   It might take
its head at an ugly turn and unseat you.   So much for our
" saxon " Parliament.—But is it likely that you *will* introduce a
healthy measure ?   That is the next question.   And that can be
answered only by looking at your record, and the leading quality
of your mind.   And when all is said and done, what you will
propose we can only *infer ;* we cannot prophesy.—

Our inferences are contained in the next section.

[1] You may be interested, though "surprised," to learn that I consistently
refuse to avail myself of the right to vote—for two or three reasons, of which
one is—that I would never, even by appearance, countenance the making of
Englishmen *cowards*.   The saxons among us are only too prone to be cowardly ;
a healthy community would make short work of the statesman who could
propose that in order to exercise their political functions, men should first and
foremost show themselves unworthy of the name of men.   (You remember
the pother at the Crewe Railway Works, before the last election.)   No honourable, fearless man ought to vote otherwise than *openly*.

[2] And *that* it will, on any measure which you propose (even *you*), which it
understands, and which is distasteful to it.   How significant that you, an aged
statesman,—" or hear'st thou rather" *an old parliamentary hand*—blundered
on the subject of the *beer* of the working man, and received prompt chastisement
for your blunder !

III.

YOUR RELATION TO THE DIFFICULTY.

Why is it that
Ireland, going
before—from
well to better,
is, under *you*,
ever going
from ill to
worse?

When I go back in thought to the Ireland of 1850–60, it presents itself to my mind as a very heaven compared with the Ireland of the present time. Whence the change? How comes it that an England becoming, by this or that "great measure," every day more and more "free,"—following with ever-increasing devotion "Liberal" principles,—championing the "rights of man" all the world over,—"sympathizing" with oppressed nationalities,—nervously alive to its "duties,"—above all, profoundly convinced of the necessity of "healing," "just," "generous" measures towards Ireland, has had such a sorry record of success? What has made Ireland what it is now—a very hell to live in, a country in three-fourths of which life, liberty, property, are of no account; where credit no longer exists, where a compact is broken with a jeer at the fool who believed in it; and where to be a friend of England brings a man more danger and loss than if he committed the foulest murder in open day? I wonder what *your* explanation of this phenomenon would be. The chatter about past misgovernment, penal laws, rack-rents, landlordism, Protestant ascendency, will not serve. In 1860, say, the Upas tree still flourished and the landowner was a burden; "sentences of death" in the shape of eviction-warrants (or whatever they are called) were passed and rigidly carried out, to the great advantage, I may remark, not only of the community at large, but (and necessarily) of the evicted themselves. Contracts were fulfilled, credit was good, stocks were rising in value, wealth among the well-doing was accumulating on every hand, resources were being developed. To say that the wolf was lying down with the lamb, that the two races and the two religions were on very cordial terms with each other, would be untrue. And no man who knew Ireland, who saw how closely the line of cleavage in respect of race coincided with the line of cleavage in respect of religion, and who understood the Celtic tendency to *certain forms* of crime (which forms may be

studied in *Giraldus Cambrensis*, who wrote before the English
Conquest), could or would expect a perfectly smooth working of
the political and social machinery,—especially in a case in which
the Government was (as it was to some extent even then) committed to *sansculotte*-humanitarian principles and methods. And
there was, no doubt, the danger that arose from what people
called " progress,"—I mean political " progress " in England—a
process which, beginning in healthy constitutionalism, degenerated
(as it must always do, save in a very robust community) into mere
party wrestling for power. But when all is said that can be
said, the truth remains, that the Ireland of 1860 was an Ireland
which seemed to be on the upward path of civilization ; and that
the idea of separation from England would have been thought
the offspring of a disordered imagination. And all this *after* past
misgovernment, nay,—if we will believe our present " leaders,"—
when " high-sighted tyranny still ranged on." Now, sir, this
was, in brief, the state of things in the Ireland of 1860 ; you
have got to say why the Ireland of our day cannot be retained
on this side of Revolution as an integral portion of the British
Empire. What your explanation would be I cannot divine—I cannot imagine. But pending *your* explanation I give *my* explanation.
And with my explanation you will have to reckon when you come
to give yours. I affirm, then (and I want the future historian
to hear me), that the difference between the Ireland of to-day
and the Ireland of 1860 is due solely and absolutely to *your*
activity, which, of course, the English Parliament and people
participated in and are therefore responsible for.

That is my assertion—disprove it if you can. And I further
affirm that the agitation to which you are about to sacrifice the
well-being, nay, the very existence, of your country, is *in origin*
a bogus agitation—without force or substance, save what has been
given to it by the petty party exigencies and the craven fears of a
set of fools, cowards, and hypocrites—who, under one name or
another, have of late years administered the government of
degenerate England. But though the agitation was in origin a
bogus, a sham agitation, and is at the present moment, *intrinsically*,
a sham of shams, yet England—because she has been content to
consult her own ease, to be ignorant, cowardly, wicked, hypo-

D

critical,—because she has spurned her real duties, because she
has acted with insolent injustice[1] in order to quiet this sham
agitation—will pay down (and herein lies the bitterest part of
her punishment) will pay down—to a *sham*—her treasure, her
blood, her prestige, her Empire—as if this sham, this sorry
phantom, were an irresistible reality! It has seemed, indeed,
for some years, as if "Christ and his Saints slept," as they were
supposed to have done in the reign of Stephen; but Christ and
his Saints—in nineteenth-century phrase, the Equities of the
Universe—neither slumber nor sleep. Retribution is upon us!—

For these among other reasons:— you are the first Minister to legislate for her—

Passing on now to discuss *your* special activity in this matter, I
will first call attention to a few points in which your mental and
moral attitude towards the question—and therefore, of course, your
actions—your policy—have differed from those of your predecessors,—the points of difference being such as to pile up obstacle
upon obstacle, not only in *your own* way, but in the way of *every
English statesman* who touches this question, now or hereafter.
The wrong has been done, and will not disappear with the
wrongdoer.

in deliberate defiance of Natural Law (..)economic;

1. You are the first responsible Minister of the Crown who, since
the adamantine laws of Political Economy were ascertained and
established, has deliberately set aside—spurned—those laws.[2] It
is the fashion just now to speak slightingly of the ("so-called")
laws of Political Economy. Very well: believe me, the laws of
Political Economy are quite able to take care of themselves. And
the community which for any reason—I do not say, *despises* them
—but fails rigidly to *follow* them through thick and thin—against
all temptation,—that community may safely be left to the inevitable consequences of its action. You—and England through
you—perpetrated a gross offence against these laws in 1881: and
now, in 1886, you and England are face to face with the Irish

---

[1] ὕβρις—that is the word which best describes the attitude of saxon England
to the *well-affected* in Ireland. She has done her best to annihilate them.
Very well; *their* annihilation will involve *hers* also—δόξα τῷ Θεῷ !

[2] I wonder how many members of this parliament (surely the most ridiculous,
and also the most mischievous, body of men that ever assembled for the purpose
of legislating!) could explain the meaning of the word "law" in the text.

Difficulty intensified a hundredfold by your own act.[1]   Do *you*
share the contempt which many of your followers profess for the
laws of Political Economy?   Apparently you do.   In your acts
you do.   Anyhow, you have sinned against them, as with a cart-
rope ; and now you are face to face with (what every sinner meets
with sooner or later)— punishment !

2. As you have been the first to legislate in the teeth of (ii.) social ;
economic principles, so you have been the first to sin openly
against the general laws of Nature—as these manifest themselves
in human society.   This offence is closely connected with the
former—the sin against economic principle.   Either offence

---

[1] Your Irish Secretary of those days, poor Mr. Forster (for whom I have a
sincere regard), whose career as statesman was so suddenly cut short, defended
your 1881 iniquity by explaining that the Irish landlords had the "pull of the
market." Very well : in 1886 you are found attempting to "square" the
landlords with a bribe of many, many millions, and *in doing so* and by doing
so—to smash the Empire. Yes : the "Laws" of Political Economy *can*
take care of themselves.—Alas, sir, since I wrote the foregoing note, that
excellent man, W. E. Forster, has passed away. He was the last of the Irish
Secretaries who worthily represented England. All his successors in the
Secretaryship have been the sorriest set of administrative *curs* that the world
has seen. (Please observe, in calling the Irish Secretaries *curs*—I am not
vituperative—I write in cool blood. What I mean is—that all the Secretaries
since Mr. Forster have been *nominally* the representatives of English power,
but *really* the slaves of *Irish* rebellion. For so far, they are *cross-breeds*. But
if you go on to add a strain of (mistaken) Christianity and of French Revolutionism—surely we are within "measurable distance" of the cur ?)—Poor
Mr. Forster ! a most pathetic figure !—a man who, like Mr. Goschen (*he* is,
happily, spared to us) *all but touched* greatness. His vice in politics was—
that he did not *think widely*,—that he mistook *symptoms* for *essentials*. His
pernicious "Education Act" will be severely handled by the historian of our
time. But I plead with the historian to mitigate his sentence as regards *the
man*. His activity was, I acknowledge, mischievous in the highest degree. *He
ruined Education in England.* But he was very ignorant of politics and of
the laws of society—even of those laws which have been long since ascertained.
On the other hand, he was a man of grand *simplicity* of character, of candour,
of indomitable courage ! By the way, sir, *you* would have consulted your own
interest had you on that sad day of Mr. Forster's death—sad to me, and sad
to thousands of Englishmen, made *some* reference—no matter how short—to
what was, in fact, a *national* calamity. In *neglecting* such things you give the
enemy occasion to blaspheme. And surely, on hearing of Mr. Forster's death
you must have remembered Burke's noble words on a similar occasion,—have
seen the hollowness of party triumphs, and felt "*what shadows we are and
what shadows we pursue !*"

denotes a certain "flabby" type of mind and character. It usually shows itself in the form of a desire to enlarge the functions of government, by laying on the State the duty of making the citizens *comfortable.* If citizens have "grievances"—even of the needy-knife-grinder sort—they are to be *"redressed."* In short, *sentiment* invades a region as far removed from it, in *the nature of things,* as is the region of the Calculus. Government is no longer a machine—(it is at best, indeed, a very clumsy and inefficient machine)—for the protection of property : Government now, all aglow with philanthropy, will arrange a happy family party ! The poor must be "raised," "educated," fed ; the peasant must be "rooted in the soil," &c. [You see we are here within touching distance of the man-and-brother fallacy.] In matter of fact, the assumption by the State of such duties amounts to the grossest tyranny ; and *we live under such a tyranny.* Well, but when we, the State, *take on* these additional and utterly irrelevant functions. what happens ? We only make things worse ! for every step we take is in flat opposition to Natural Law, and as such, must be attended with danger, loss, disaster. But many (especially the flabby Rights-of-man philanthropists) deny that such Law exists. Excellent ! "The fool hath said in his heart—there is no God." When we go about to break a law, nothing like denying the existence of that law ! But if there is no law, let us look at *fact.*— You presided over an organisation whose *sole* function, I am prepared to prove, is *to protect property* all over the British Empire. You took on the *additional* function of making the Irish tenants *comfortable, happy.*[1] Now let us see how you set about making the Irish tenants comfortable, happy—and the *result* of your efforts.

---

[1] I protest it is enough to make a saint swear to see the blundering *gauche* attempts of the brutal, dull, pudding-headed saxons to make happy—as superior persons, the bright, sensitive Celt !—the Celt, who enjoys life in one year—living as he often does on a dinner (and I ought to know, for I have shared it with him !) of *petates and salt*—more than the saxon Sir Gorgias Midas in his whole dull-as-dishwater existence ! But the courses of the last twenty years have soured the Celt. He is now dour, ungracious, suspicious ; even the English accent puts his back up.—Yet we live in the era of "generous" measures,—of "enlightened" statesmanship ! But when I think of the Celt of to-day and the Celt of thirty years ago, I am constrained to wish enlightened statesmanship—at the devil.

In order to compass this object you were compelled at once to engage in a course of *plunder:* that is, to violate deliberately the primary law of your being! You existed to *protect* property, and you were allowed to use "force as a remedy" against those degenerate members of the community who would rob others of their property. But you turned aside from—nay, abjured altogether—your obligation to protect the plundered man, and—yourself, the English Government—became his chief plunderer! And the end of this fine sentimental way of governing is at hand. You would make the Irish tenants happy: you would "root the peasant in the soil."[1] To make the peasant happy you plundered his landlord. And *yet* the peasant is not happy. *Now* you are going to square the landlord, and to do so you must plunder the people of England—to wrest from them as much as was expended in building up the British Empire. Do you think the landlord will, "after all," be as happy as if you had contented yourself, in the government of Ireland, with such a non-sentimental course as the mere enforcing of contract? That was all you *could* do healthily—all you were permitted by the Laws of Nature to do. And *had you done that*, Kerry would now be as peaceable as Kent. There is an equity, you see, in the nature of things. We English passed and applauded your grand "healing" measure, and we stood by while your bandit-commissioners were bog-trotting all over Ireland, "fixing *fair* rents"! The curse has come home to us. It is just that it should; we must pay *somehow;* but do you think *we* are happy?—And lastly, are *you* happy?

3. You were, I think, the first to regard *Crime* as a thing demanding any treatment other than Punishment. Irish Crime (which is usually of a peculiarly hellish type[2]) you regarded as an

and in encouragement of— (iii.) crime;

---

[1] As to the *wisdom* of this policy see Section IV.

[2] I say advisedly *Irish* crime. The Celt does not take to certain sorts of crime which are to the saxon as the breath of his nostrils. For example, you find no wife-kicking among the Celts. In short the Celt is *sensitive*—in some respects morbidly so—to the extent of pepperiness; the saxon is not. But the Celt has a very undeveloped conscience, say, rather an embryonic conscience, even if *that;* therefore his criminal acts, while they shock us by their devilish wickedness, seem *unaccountable* on any grounds other than the supposition that the perpetrators were *mad.* Take the case of the Joyce murders, the Phœnix Park murders, the Sheehan murders, the murder of Finlay the process-server, then the treatment of the Curtins,—of the widow of Finlay, &c., &c.

evidence of political discontent,—to be met by "Concessions" [*see* Lie 10, p. 15], as if a man who, under any circumstances, could commit a crime could, under any circumstances, or by any "concessions," be made a good citizen.   Give one of the men who murdered Lord Mountmorres, or who danced in his blood, *sixpence a week* (the amount of reduction effected by your grand Land Act of 1881),[1] and he at once becomes well-affected towards England, and a worthy member of society !   Such, in effect, is your theory. Of course this tolerance towards crime is a "note" of the "flabbiness" of modern England.   Criminals are spoken of as the "victims" of our social condition !   But if crime—crime of a purely political character, and committed to further political ends —is to be taken as evidence that political "concessions" are required (—and again, if "force is no remedy")—*why did you hang Joe Brady?*   No, sir, crime is crime.   And it would have been far healthier, and in every way better, if Ireland had, after the murder of Lord Frederick Cavendish, been governed as a Penal Settlement for ten years :—a sentiment, of course, which does not commend itself to modern *sansculotte*-humanitarianism ; but then, that same humanitarianism is a "note" of our national *decay*.

and (iv.) separation.   4. You have been the first to carry "concession" to the point of absolute *surrender*, to weaken *vitally* the tie binding Ireland to England, and to expect,[2] or, at least, to *affirm*, that the connection would be closer and more cordial !   But here again you are inconsistent.   How comes it that your "concessions" were not made once for all ?   What it is right to concede now, it was surely right to concede in 1870 ?   And if Ireland is to be governed by Irish ideas, and you go in for "concession," why don't you "concede" all that the vast majority of the accredited representatives of Ireland demand ? Why don't you settle this business out of hand by *following absolutely* the directions of Mr. Parnell ?   Why come to me or any "other discreet and learned" outsider, "and open your grief"? Behold your master !   But now, has it ever occurred to you that

---

[1] *Sixpence a week*—that is the average to the agricultural population *per head* —secured by your Land Act.

[2] At least rhetorically. I am utterly unable to follow your *logic*. But perhaps you don't intend that there should be any logic to follow ?   Perhaps it is *all* rhetoric ?   I fear this is the view of the case taken by the Fates.   *Qui vivra verra.*   *I* have no doubt on the subject.

this word "concession"—though it looks kind, and Christian, and "all that sort of thing"—is in reality a very dangerous word ? Ask yourself what exactly it stands for in your mind. *My* account of it is this :—I owe a man money. I pay him. *That* is not concession. I don't owe him any money, and in spite of his threats and howls I *refuse* to pay him. *That* is not concession. I don't owe him, *yet I pay him : that* is "concession." But for my part, I can't for the life of me see where or how this "concession" comes in properly in connection with public affairs.—You and I find ourselves among a body of selfish brutes fighting for their tickets at a railway ticket-office window. I, being first on the ground, have the right to get my ticket before you ; but you are an old man, and I "concede" to you the privilege which I possess : I allow you to get your ticket before me, and I take my chance of finding a comfortable seat in a crowded train. I understand concession here. But I don't understand "concession" in a case, say, in which I am the guardian of an orphan, and that orphan's patrimony is threatened with serious diminution or actual extinction by the exorbitant charges of a scoundrel-lawyer who has been employed to protect it. I must fight that scoundrel. It is a sacred duty. And if he resists, I must show him that Force *is* a remedy. Now this latter case presents, I hold, the analogue to the position of the statesman. I regret, sir, to have to say that in your public policy you always seem to be the champion, advocate, and friend of every country but your own.[1] Yet I

[1] And it is therefore in no wise to be wondered at that your accession to power is always hailed with delight in quarters in which praise of an English statesman ought to give that statesman pause—ought to lead that statesman to ask whether he has always consulted the true interests of his country. You are in high favour in the offices of the *Novoe Vremya* and the *Vedomosti :* for my part, I should feel my earnings much safer and my income-tax more of a stationary, (certainly not an *increasing*), quantity, if you had the good word of the Berlin *Post,* of the *Nord-deutsche Allgemeine Zeitung,* or of the Vienna *Freie Presse* and *Fremdenblatt.* It is amusing to observe that the journals of your "party" in this country reproduce the acclaims of the *Novoe Vremya Vedomosti* and Brussels *Nord,* as if they were solid testimonials to your merit ! Is this *naiveté,* or do your able editors accurately gauge their public ?—Since writing this note, and on the very day—big with fate !—on which you are to make your proposals—at least the *first* of them—the *Daily News,* which I read regularly, prints a paragraph from its Odessa correspondent, containing

think you will—in theory—admit that your duty when you are
Prime Minister of England is, first and foremost, to England.[1]
Very well·—in that case, what is the meaning of "concession"?
You may concede—ruin, burn, sink, and destroy what is *your own*
—as I can concede to you my right of being served before you
with a railway-ticket. But I don't see how you, as first Minister
of the Crown, can "concede" to any other country that which
belongs of right to England—to England, and not *to you.*—You
made a final "concession" to Ireland in carrying through your
"great" Land Bill of 1881. A *concession* you *called* it. But
wherein did the "concession" consist? You beggared the landowners in Ireland by form of law, in order to conciliate the Irishry.
And you did so *under pressure* from this same Irishry.   You
called that "concession": I called it then, and I call it now, rank
injustice, villany,—and hypocrisy into the bargain. *You—England*
—conceded nothing—sacrificed nothing that was *yours—England's.*
You deliberately ruined one class that was loyal, law-abiding, and
England-loving, in order to please, and (as you hoped —such is
your ignorance of the Irish character—) to satisfy and pacify

"Russian views on Mr. Gladstone's Irish Policy." And among these "views"
are some very impudent anticipations as to what will happen, should "the
Sovereign exercise a prerogative inimical to a dissolution by Mr. Gladstone."
Public opinion (*i.e.* "saxon" opinion) would, it seems, triumphantly "support and carry the great Liberal leader and reformer (meaning *you*, though the
word *reformer* is a strange word in this connection) over all obstacles," &c.
Could anything surpass this in the quality of *naïveté*—or something else ?—
But the *feature* of this issue of the *Daily News* is a copy of verses under the
heading "At Last."—They prove conclusively that the art of writing the
rhyming pentameter is not yet a lost art. Of course, one does not expect a
poet to be a politician. The *substance* of this poem is sad stuff. But what
of that? If "glorious John" is once more amongst us —that is something
to be thankful for. The verses are evidently by the same hand that lately
offered some very severe "poetical" strictures on you, sir, to the editor of the
St. James's Gazette. That gentleman rejected them. I hope he now sees his
mistake.

[1] Perhaps you wouldn't. Perhaps you would say you must act as the Friend-
of-humanity. In that case my argument, of course, falls to the ground. But
I can tell you that the statesman who avails himself of his position to play the
rôle of *Friend-of-humanity*, will very soon be cast by Fate as *Enemy-of-his-
country.* For my part, I contribute to support the public burdens only on the
understanding that public men will look after *my* interests, and *not* the interests
of Afghan, Turk, or *Russian.*

those who live only to hate England. And now, you are once more on the war-trail (pardon the figure): you are for the third time face to face with the "final settlement" of the Irish Difficulty. And "the way and means thereto is"—concession! You are going to concede a "large and generous" measure of county government, or, it may be (—and at present writing your followers are all abroad as to what they will have to vote for), a Parliament in Dublin. Either measure is fraught, and *equally* fraught, with (virtual) *death* to England. Here, indeed, England *does* sacrifice something solid—her hegemony, namely, in these islands and her Empire abroad. There is here no hypocrisy (unless you should maintain that you are, by your measure, *strengthening* the Union); but is not this too much to pay for any *possible*, any *conceivable* advantage you would reap from concession? —*Now*, perhaps, you understand why I am not very much taken with "concession,"—word or thing.

5. You were the first—so far as I know—to employ a certain peculiar phraseology—language—mode of expression—in English politics. The proverb tells us that "hard words break no bones," but words count for something when they are addressed to the "saxon" in the House of Commons or out of doors. For the saxon among us, in Parliament or out of it, is only at "that-blessed-word-Mesopotamia" stage of intellectual development. He does not distinguish between the *real* and the *rhetorical*. He does not weigh—very often he does not understand—the words addressed to him. Hence the solid *danger* to the saxon, to you, to me, to all of us.—This peculiar mode of expression may be described thus: You perform, or are about to perform (or commit), a certain act. That act would be in the Queen's English designated by a certain term: now, *select the contrary* —or, indeed, take *anything* as *if it were* the contrary (with the saxon it matters not) of that term—and the trick is done.— Propose a measure of *robbery*—of *spoliation*: but say not a word about robbery, about spoliation! Call it an *act of justice*. If a devoted servant of England (of whom the England of our time was not worthy) is in sore straits—beholding with his physical eyes, nothing but enemies only too physical, with rifles in their hands, on all sides of him,—rebuke with Christian warmth the

[side note: You are the first, too, to practise deliberately— (v.) on the saxon, by perversion of language ;]

presumptuous person who dares to say that this devoted servant
of England is *surrounded ;* and when you have mastered your
indignation (—you do well to be angry), condescend to explain
that this devoted servant of England is NOT *surrounded,* he is
only *hemmed in.* When, again, you disgrace an able and courageous officer,—another devoted servant and representative of
England—by recalling him at a most critical moment (—and, let
me tell you, the Central Asian Question is *not yet* " settled "),
repel with indignation the charge that you *recalled* this distinguished public servant, and affirm that he was only requested
" *to repair to the metropolis.*" And in regard to this Irish Question
—if your policy *manifestly* should be to grant all-round " concession " to the Irishry—all that you think will satisfy them,—and
to abase, rob, annihilate " your own flesh and blood " in Ireland—
you must disarm all opposition by assuring Parliament that your
policy was a policy of strict impartiality, and launching into
nautical figure, you must exclaim that you were determined, as
between one Irishman and another, to " *steer an even keel*"—
an even keel!—when, in *fact,* you were carrying on with *three
planks under* to leeward.—I declare I am here in the presence of a mystery ; and I am not good at solving mysteries.
I cannot—no, I *cannot,* after long trying—see how you could,
for example, call your Land Bill of 1881, an *act of justice*—an
act of justice !—but I give it up. *Davus sum, non Œdipus.* Your
political opponents have an off-hand way of explaining such
mysteries. They travel into the region of the *moral,* and affirm
that *there* the explanation of the mystery lies. I don't follow
them into that region. But I don't say they are wrong. I only
say that it is an additional mystery if a round dozen of English
statesmen and many others, not statesmen, but—" all, all, honourable men," [1] could conspire to affirm *the thing that is not.* Perhaps

---

[1] When your Land Bill was going through the Houses, a distinguished
Churchman preached a sermon, in which (—so the *Daily News* reported)
he quoted a celebrated peroration of yours beginning " *Justice must be our
guide.*" An act of gigantic breach of faith is committed, and *Dux Justitia
facti !*—the virtue of Justice personified guides you to measures which ten years
before you denounced as " spoliation." *Spoliation,* 1870—*Justice,* 1881 !
Mystery on mystery !

they looked only to their *motives ?* But I won't attempt to fathom this mystery either.[1] I am of that "uncultured" class of persons who have not the "insight" to call a spade anything but—a spade ; and who (such our *Beschränctheit*—our narrowness of view) could never see in a *spade* a pound of sugar or a railway locomotive ! This, by the way, must be my apology for many expressions you will find in this paper. " I am a plain man, I can not gloze."

6. Lastly, you have been the first English statesman to succumb to an agitation that was *absolutely* of his own creation. I have called this Irish agitation a sham agitation ; intrinsically it is a sham of shams. I now affirm that *you* (—" with the best intentions ") called it into being, and have nurtured and coddled it till it is, this day, fit to strangle both you and the British Empire " without handling a gun." A sham in inception, it may be bracketed with the "saxon" in the midst of us, as far and away the most dangerous enemy we have to face. For one thing, we could not, as a people, even set about meeting it without resorting to violent reactionary measures ; and every wise statesman abhors violence and abhors reaction. And then we must ask, Have we, as a people, courage to resort to violence and to adopt reactionary courses, even where our very existence is at stake ? The saxon is our master. Anyhow, this state of things, sir, we owe absolutely to you—always admitting (which I do ungrudgingly) the fell complicity of England ;—England which has permitted you to blunder on this Irish Question, to blunder even when your former blunders, gross and palpable, were being visited with their natural consequences, and when you (one would have thought) were *found out*—and which has again and again called you in

—and (vi)on the Celt, with sham grievances and by sham agitation ending up in the sham becoming absolutely —master.

---

[1] That a large body of men, all reputed upright, and some of them by profession pious—and paid handsome salaries for merely doing their best or going through a decent and for the greater part prescribed *form* of doing their best to make other people pious—should contrive to select within a certain region words which I do not say *misdescribe* the things they are supposed to stand for, but accurately describe their *opposites*—this is a fact that must be taken into account by every student of our social and political condition. This inversion of terms is strange—startling,—but not unprecedented. Isaiah (v. 20, 21, 23) notices the same phenomenon in his time. " *Woe unto them that call evil good, and good evil ; that put darkness for light, and light for darkness ; that put bitter for sweet, and sweet for bitter,*" &c., &c.

to put still further from right what you had already disastrously
put wrong—*that* England will not fail of her deserts: retribution will
be upon her soon—as I have already said,—is, in fact, upon her
now. But you, sir, were the cause of the evil—in the sense that
if a statesman of the right stamp (—I can name no such public
man in England : for the good reason that modern England
would not allow the *right* man to become a *public* man) had held
the reins of power during the last twenty years, the evil would not
now exist : there would be no Irish party threatening you within
an inch of your life, if you don't make your, *i.e.* England's,
approaching surrender humiliating enough, *absolute* enough ; and
the Irish Question would be every day tending of itself towards
a peaceful solution. While, if this right man in the right place
had had, during the same time, a *worthy* England at his back,
an England worthy to possess that glorious island, with its
easily-governed Celtic population—easily governed, I say, but *only
by the right* man—why, sir, in that case (—and how much every
lover of Ireland and of England must regret that this is but a
vision, and that he must "put the vision by"!)—the Irish
Difficulty would now be hastening to make itself a bit of *real*
"ancient history."

*You are thus
the creator of
the Irish
party.*

Of the "Irish party"—brought into existence by you, spoonfed
by you, educated, supported by you, and now about to receive
from you—"the Governor," the share of goods that falleth to
them and to go their way,—of this party—*as* a party—I must
speak in terms of admiration—in so far as I must admire
magnificent discipline, shining intellectual ability, no matter
how or in what cause displayed. That is all that I can in
conscience say of a party whose activity is, and must be, fraught
with nothing but evil to Ireland. Anyhow, they certainly form
a striking contrast to the parcel of *Gurths*[1] sent up by the new

---

[1] And Gurth, we know, was the son of Beowulph, *the born thrall* of Cedric
of Rotherwood, and a *born thrall* he is of *somebody* to the present hour. But
Gurth was a very dull fellow. For my part, since Parliamentary proceedings
have now taken on so much of the character of a *farce*, I want the piece to
be consistently played *as such !*—and could well have spared our chaw-bacon
Gurths if we had in their room and stead the descendants of "Wamba, the son
of Witless, the son of Weatherbrain, the son of an alderman"! The piece
would then *go.* For example, I read *every word* of Mr. Labouchere's speeches,

constituencies. These must, I should think, remind members
of the Irish party who served in former Parliaments of the
twenty-nine Ulster " dead-heads" whereof so few have had
an opportunity of revisiting the glimpses of the electric light on
the Clock Tower at Westminster.—The present Irish Parliamentary party is unquestionably a magnificent machine! I am
inclined to think, sir, that it is the finest thing you have ever
done in the way of "constructive statesmanship." Behold
the phalanx of the enemies you have reared; young they are,
lusty, vigorous—masters of Parliamentary tactics, though many of
them have not been in Parliament for as many weeks as you
have been years—silent as the grave when the word is passed
that silence is the *lay*—again, solemnly persuasive, discursive,
talkative, tedious— exasperating— when the *mot-d'ordre* is —
"*Occupy time.*" But *in every case*, the saxon line, bulging ever more
and more inwards, attests the strategical and tactical ability of
the leaders, and the brilliant soldiership of the rank and file.

Yet they too hasten to their *Sédan ;* and their fall will come in
the moment of their triumph. Their offence is rank. I admit
that what constituted their offence has placed them in the
position they now occupy—that of the *real* arbiters of the destiny
of the British Empire. I admit that the temptation to win this
position was great : *but they fell,* and no mere intellectual gifts can
atone for *moral* delinquency. Be that as it may (I will discuss
their offence presently), they now have their grip on the throat of
England, and can choke her off Ireland when they please. And

—a party whose doings, like your own—whose success !!!—a dire Nemesis, awaits :

also of those of the *Irish* members ; and it is to me, sir, somewhat of a
trial that *you* are not a bit *funny.*—Pray don't call me flippant. Don't
reprove me as you reprove your colleague in the cartoon of the Augurs. I
jest, because I am *very much* in earnest. And what makes me very much in
earnest is this : that Parliamentary Government, *by your insanity* in the matter
of the Franchise, has broken down in England, and become discredited all
the world over ! Prince Bismarck (the only *great* statesman of our time) points
—and justly—to England as the temperance lecturer pointed to his "*awful
example.*"—Do *you* relish that ? I don't. I am ashamed, confounded, ex-
asperated.—*Now,* which is the more serious—the man who *deliberately* with
a light heart—gaily—makes a certain form of government—the most civilised
yet evolved—*ridiculous—contemptible,* or the man who in sheer bitterness of
spirit does his best to laugh the ridiculous thing off the stage ?

choke her off they will.—By the by, I hope you are not mis-
led in this matter by a certain quality in your mind which has
often led you astray, a sort of vague, hazy, dreamy optimism ;—
I hope you have not argued yourself into believing that you can
have Home Rule in any shape or form consistent with the
"integrity of the Empire." *Home Rule means Separation*—that,
and nothing else. The more timid, feeble members of your
following, when they presume to canvass your divine plans, hope
you will introduce a "large and generous" measure of local self-
government in the shape of County Boards, &c. ; [1] that is their
way of saying that they hope you *won't* propose an Irish Parliament in Dublin. But the one measure is for them, for you, for
England, as fatal as the other; either means Separation. And
the Irish party "go for" that, and nothing short of that.

But then will come their Nemesis. In what form ?—Well, hard
and stupid things are *said* of them. They will, however, survive
all mere malignity and all mere stupidity. Their fate does not
depend on what is said of them.—They are described, for example,
as a set of "low fellows" who live upon the contributions of their
congeners (often called their "dupes") on the other side of the
Atlantic, and of as many as "seventeen nationalities" besides.
And a noble Duke lately affirmed that what they receive as salary,
they spend in drunkenness and debauchery in London. It is true
this last statement was afterwards withdrawn handsomely enough,
—but it is one of those statements which ought never to have
been made. It was a libel. But it was also an irrelevancy. Is

---

[1] And one would think, to hear these Gladstonian conies discuss the question,
that a "generous measure of local self-government " is what they have been
pining for all their lives—the truth being that this County Board scheme denotes
a mere *bulging of the line :* it is a thing they would never have thought of but
for *United Ireland's* demand for a Parliament in Dublin. But County Boards
with an Irish party in Westminster, or a Parliament in Dublin, with no representatives in Westminster—which would *United Ireland* prefer? The
County Board scheme (with your, the Gladstonian, franchise) will deliver up
to the Irishry the few capitalists left (the landowners need not be taken into
account), and they will still be able to put their hands into the pockets of the
English taxpayer and make him pay "ransom "—for nothing. (And serve *him*
right.) On the other hand, a Parliament in Dublin would satisfy "*national*"
sentiment. This arrangement would cost money ; and where could the money
be found ?

it insinuated that the Irish party don't do their duty? Well! anybody who knows the House of Commons knows that there is not, and never has been, a party more assiduous, more hard-working, than the Irish party under the *magnificent* leadership of Mr. Parnell.[1] And those who know the party as individuals know how absurd is the imputation of drunkenness and debauchery.[2] —But I take other ground. In regard to the Irish party's dependence on money contributed by the American-Irish and their friends of "seventeen nationalities" in America, I wish to remark, and my reason is plain, that where there is smoke there is fire; and that if the American-Irish (even "servant girls") give their dollars to support the Irish party in the English Parliament,[3] this shows that we have got a very *earnest* foe to contend with.[4] But I affirm, that never was money expended (—I don't sympathize with the Irish party, but truth is truth) more effectually than that which the American-Irish have expended on the "Irish party." The American-Irish have desired a certain article : I don't say they were wise in desiring it ; but that is not the question. Well, the "Irish party" have got it for them. *Que leur faut-il de plus ?*

Then, as to drunkenness and debauchery. Even if the "Irish" members *are* drunken and debauched—that is none of our business. I have nothing to do with the morals of public men any more than I have with their shirt-collars.[5] I never inquire whether you, for example, are in private life a monster of asceticism, an angel of sweetness and light,—or a very *very* wicked old gentleman. I regard you exactly as I regard the steersman at the wheel on board a steamer in which I may happen to be a passenger. I don't want to "speak"

[1] Mr. Parnell will of course very soon have to get out of the way. The pace will become too fast even for *him.*

[2] I can't quote the Duke of Westminster's exact words, for I write at a distance from books, newspapers, &c., and have, besides, no time to consult them. But if I misreport what the Duke said I hope somebody will correct me.

[3] Mr. T. P. O'Connor affirms the Irish party can get £5,000 a week if they want it. I *think* that is the sum he mentioned.

[4] When would our saxon knock off his 'backy and his beer, were it to chain Satan for a thousand years ?

[5] *Your* shirt-collars, sir, I leave to Harry Furniss and your washerwoman. I have, and take, as little to do with your morals.

to the man at the wheel.[1]   I don't care what his views on the
Liquor Question are.   I don't want to know whether he is married
or single.   I have nothing to do with his theology, his politics,
his morals, or his opinion on the question whether life is worth
living.   He is at the wheel : very well, I want him to steer
efficiently, so that I shall get soon and safe to the end of the
voyage.   He may drink his fill in his watch below, and, for the
matter of that, even when he is on duty, provided the liquor *will
make him steer better.*   For my part, I could be well content to see
at the present juncture the helm of the State in the hand of such a
man as Lucius Cornelius Sulla—and there certainly was no strait-
lacedness about *him.*   But he could *steer.*[2]—This prying, nudging-
and-winking, eyebrow-raising curiosity is, in fact, another mark of
the " flabbiness " of our time, as it was a mark of the Athenian in his
decay.   And the people who talk about the Irish members in this
fashion resemble nothing so much as a blackguard corner-boy, who,
when you box his ears for some offence against public decency, calls
you all sorts of *quite irrelevant* bad names because he can do nothing
else.—Then we hear reports of *divisions* in the Irish party—reports
circulated and greedily listened to by those to whom such intelligence would be very welcome.   The Irish party won't split up
to please these people.   The split will come, but it will be only
after the Irish party have very effectually " split " the Empire.   No :
the Irish party will survive mere envy, calumny, and irrelevant
chatter.   No man and no body of men are ever permanently
affected by such things.   The only way the Irish party can be put
down is—by all English parties being as efficient and as determined to frustrate their designs as *they* are to carry them out.

[1] I don't want even *to see* him.   And I certainly would never attend Hawarden
Church when you read the Lessons, for I might be confounded with the gaping
herd of vulgarians (saxons, every man of them) who trouble your peace on
the Sabbath.

[2] From the man-and-brother point of view, I might wish the steersman
didn't indulge *quite* so freely.   But I hope you begin to perceive that *statesmanship* has got nothing to do with man-and-brother theories.   Our main
concern in statesmanship is—*our* national *safety.*   From *this* point of view, and
given the *conditions* (suppose, *e.g.*, the ship in danger—this the only steersman,
and alcohol with him an hourly necessity), I can picture Sir Wilfrid himself
busily engaged in preparing the steersman's dram—" neat "—" cold without "
—or " 'ot with "—as he might desire.   Oh—we are *such* hypocrites !

The advantage of *numbers* is all against them ; and we surely live under the blessed dispensation of the rule of the Majority.

But I have said that the Irish party, as representing the Irishry —will one day meet with a terrible reverse. Now, it is curious that the reverse will be complete *only* when they obtain the very summit of their ambition, which is, of course, Separation.[1] And by how much they fall short of attaining *that* object of their dreams and labours, by so much will they be able *in a certain set of circumstances* to mitigate the evils attendant on that shattering defeat. Absolute success and absolute ruin go, for *them*, hand in hand. Assuming that they will obtain Separation—which is what they want—the reverse will then present itself to them *at once*, and in two forms. They may *avoid* defeat in the case of the first, though there is not one chance in a thousand that they will ;—before the second they *must* go down. I will explain this to you.

I. The very moment they attain Separation,—when the hated flag of England has been hauled down for the last time from the staff on the great tower of Dublin Castle—when Ireland is going to be in very deed "for the Irish," when "Irish ideas" are to have free play,—the victorious Irishry will have the "*Ulster question*" to face. How will the Irishry "settle" that question? What if Ulster rebels against the hated domination of the Celt ? "Then the bird that can sing and won't sing must be *made* to sing. We will call in the Queen's troops to coerce the rebels : we will force them to their knees." [Ominous words, *Coercion !* and *Force !* Force is, it seems, a remedy "after all."]

But, steady, Mr. Harrington ! *Ex hypothesi*, you are "free." Ireland is yours. A British regiment will, in the new order of things, be as much of an irrelevancy in Ireland as would be a battalion of the Prussian Imperial Guard. "But we will not be wholly separate from England." Very well, but, in that case, what

i.—In an Ulster that will have none of Celtic rule :

---

[1] I don't say this is Mr. Parnell's ambition. But he knows very well that the frenzy of hatred towards England which possesses the Irish Celts will have Separation and nothing but Separation. He hates England : but his hatred doesn't send him into a fit every time he hears the word England mentioned. He is cool and cautious, and will jump off the engine in time to save himself from the inevitable collision.

E

becomes of your grand idea of severing "*every link*" that binds
you to your oppressor?   And do you really think that you will
establish just such a connection as shall enable you to call in
British troops when you want to "coerce" people who are, in
spirit and *grip*, more English than the English ever were—even
in their best days ; and that England will have nothing farther
to do with Ireland?   British troops will, I suppose, go over dis-
guised—in order not to hurt the susceptibilities of the Celt—and
having "coerced"their own congeners in the North, will be smuggled
out of Ireland by a considerate Irish Government (!) as soon as possible. Well, even suppose that *were* the case. England has of late
been party to so many irrelevant villanies that I wouldn't put *that*
one "past her."   But will she be *able* to send troops to reduce the
"rebel" element in the North? If her saxon has his way, she
will require all her resources to enable her to rub on among the
states of Europe. But even suppose she were able to send
troops, and did send troops, to put down the Northern "rebels"
—rebels not to the English flag but to the *anti*-English flag, if
there could be such a thing in the Universe—suppose her troops
entering Ulster, and that they meet there, as, please God, they will,
100,000 men well-armed, disciplined, and determined? "What
do you think of *that*, my cat?"   Late events have taught us
that our troops can be beaten, and though I am no prophet,
I assert that if ever England tries by force to put down the
Ulstermen when they are thoroughly roused—to put them
under the feet of the bitterest enemies alike of them and of
England too—not to mention the abominable spectacle of the
Queen's troops shooting down the Queen's most loyal subjects
—England may find in Ulster another Majuba Hill or a Sara-
toga.—But suppose the Ulsterman beaten.[1]   Then he will put

---

[1] By the way, should things come to this pass, we may live to see the day
when Ulster, "coerced" by the saxon *Government* of Engla d (force being
here a remedy) will be supported in men and material by the *people* of England.
(They will not want *men* though : the home-made article couldn't be improved
in quality, and up to 100,000 in numbers Ulster may be relied upon.)—Will
not this look very like Civil War in England? Mr. Joseph Arch, First Lord
of the Admiralty (many things having happened since he was bothered by
English synonyms) will order Admiral Lord (or ex-Lord) Charles Beresford
to keep a strict watch on all vessels between "the Mull" and Innishowen Head

Ulster under the protection of the United States. And suppose they won't have him—then he will piecemeal clear out, and bring his intelligence, thrift, uprightness, to a better market under the Stars and Stripes than he ever found under the "Union"-Jack.[1] But what he will *never* do is—to submit to a Celtic Parliament in any shape or form.[2]

I beg your pardon, sir; the exigencies of my argument have compelled me to address Mr. Harrington, an able lieutenant of Mr. Parnell. If all I have written in regard to Ulster is not intelligible to you, I regret it very much. But if it is not, you ought at once to make yourself acquainted with the spirit of that part of the Queen's dominions. And it may be a contribution worth making towards your study of Ulster and of the Irish Question to inform you of some leading facts. The Ulster population is quiet, orderly, law-abiding, industrious and wealth-producing. Further, the backbone of it is, in religion Presbyterian, and in politics " Liberal "—far more truly and intelligently *Liberal* than any body of English Liberals that I have ever come across.[3] The North-of-Irelanders are " Liberals "—*not* Radicals. And strange to say, sir, they have even now a profound belief in *you*.[4] The Franchise

—it having come to the knowledge of " My Lords" that military stores in large quantities were being sent from England and Scotland to the ports of Derry and Portrush, for the use of the "rebels" against the Irish Government—or it might be against " Her Majesty's" Government !

[1] Which, by the way, must now be modified. The Irish will surely never allow the Cross of St. Patrick to appear on an "alien" ensign.

[2] The only truly "Irish" Parliament was the Parliament of May, 1690—which passed attainders on Irish landowners to the number of 2,000. You see the Irish landowner has always had a bad time of it.

[3] There is a narrowness, a bigotry, a "wicked-Tory" smack about modern English " Liberalism" which is very offensive. Rather, I ought to call this " Liberalism" Latter-Day Radicalism. We see it exemplified, *e.g.*, in the gracious utterances of the sometime Rev. Thorold Rogers. Such utterances would not "take" with North-of-Ireland Liberals. Southwark is the right shop for *them*. This Radicalism, by the way, is almost the polar opposite of the original Radicalism —that of Burdett, Cochrane, Grote, Roebuck, &c.

[4] I have laboured, during recent visits among them, to detach them from two beliefs—their belief in England, and their belief in *you*. They are stern, loyal Calvinists, and cannot be moved like the saxon herd that follow you on this side.—I learn, with great satisfaction, as I pass these pages out of my hand, that they are intensely disgusted with your late manœuvrings. This is good news. Puritan Ulster is not dead, but sleepeth ! And when she awakes, you

Act of last year consigned them to political extinction; but even after you clubbed your rifle and "went for" them, they continued to believe in the soundness of your statesmanship—which did not say much, I freely admit, for the soundness of their judgment. At the same time, I think it will be granted that devotion to a political, or any other leader, even after he has taken a course that would not justify such devotion—a wrong course—a wicked course—is (most would say,) a venial fault. I must add that their being a very religious community, and your being a very religious man, has materially strengthened their feeling of regard for you. Piety is very beautiful.

But you will probably take a course one of these days which will disillusionize them.[1] You have robbed them of political weight though, *in fact*, they are the weightiest element in the population of Ireland; and they were told with brutal cynicism, when you were passing your Franchise Bill, that the English and Scotch members would represent them! Very well: but now you will rob them of their liberty by committing the blackest bit of treachery known to history: you will deliver them up, bound hand and foot by your new franchise, to their bitter enemies. That Franchise Act, which deprived them, at one blow, of political existence in so far as England is concerned, would deprive them of representation in an "Irish" Parliament if they would condescend to acknowledge such an assembly.[2] You went to the gutter for your constituency in Ireland, and you found your swarms of Celts; just as you went to the gutter in England and got your swarms of saxons. But

---

and your ferocious crew of Celtic thieves will hear of it! N.B.—I am not a Presbyterian North-of-Irelander. I speak of these things with the coolness of a zoo ogist. But *I know what I am talking about.*

[1] While writing the above sentence I have been told that your opening speech on Thursday, the 8th inst., on the Irish question, will occupy about two hours and a half. Most rhetorical sir! that speech will be *two hours* too long! *Cut it down,* why should it cumber the pages of *Hansard?* And if it be anything more than rhetoric, why should it remain to rise in judgment against you at a future day? All that you will *need* to say can be said in the margin of *half-an-hour.* See Section IV.

[2] The way the Northerners would recognise it would be—if it interfered with *them*—to march on Dublin and *break*, in the strict sense of the term, that Parliament.

there are men in these islands who are neither Celts nor saxons, and who could, if the pinch came, turn all the Celts and saxons out of them. And no men would be more efficient at such a bit of work than the hardy Presbyterians of the North of Ireland. If they are now what they were twenty years ago, you could find among them many a Joubert, many a Pretorius.[1] I warn you, sir, to take care of rousing this population by any crying injustice such as that which you may even now have decided to inflict upon it. You have deprived them of what you call the "right" of the Franchise. What Hodge, with no opinions, and little capacity to form opinions, has had thrust upon him, that the intelligent North-of-Ireland farmer, with very decidedly Liberal opinions, has been deprived of. Don't go farther and try to annihilate these Ulstermen, for *they won't be annihilated.* Their devotion does not extend so far. And you will never see them for your sake, for your comfort, for your glory—putting their necks meekly under the heel of a hated tyrant of alien blood and religion, with an "*Ave, Cæsar Imperator, morituri Te salutant.*" The Celt may have *you and the saxon* by the throat, but, by heaven, sir, he has not yet tried, and if he is wise, will never try that trick on the Northern Presbyterian;[2] for the moment the Celt, made triumphant by the brutal saxon Parliament of England through mere count of heads, comes within hitting distance of the Northerner, he will get what, in North-of-Ireland

---

[1] They succumbed, I am sorry to say, to the temptations held out to them by your Land Bill of 1881. And of late I have observed with concern a falling off in religious earnestness and a corresponding demoralisation of view in regard to the rights of property. They listened to "Liberal" orators, who told them they had rights in the land *along with* the landlord, and who went back for proofs to the terms of the arrangements made at the Plantation of Ulster from 1607 onwards. But this did not alter the *fact* that A, who rented a farm from B in, say, 1879, owed all the rent that he had *agreed to pay. It was a contract.* The North-of-Ireland farmer may now reflect that the statesman who taught him how a contract may be broken, and yet has "*good intentions*" as his motto and "*Justice*" as his guide, can go farther in faithlessness, and break his contract to protect that farmer. Then perhaps the farmer will see things in another light.—Anyhow, he will soon be "exercised" by something very different from the "*Kist-o'-whustles*" controversy.

[2] Always provided that the Northern Presbyterian population is anything like what it was when I lived in the midst of it.

phrase, *he didn't make bargain for ;* [1] and he and you will learn
that there are other forces in this Universe besides those lodged
in your great god—The Majority.

Then, sir, the Irish party will have to reckon with the Orange
Society. Those excellent young fellows who write for *United
Ireland* (and they have no more " constant " and admiring
reader than they have in me) speak of the Orangemen as the
Orange *rowdies ;* and they have—I give them all credit for
the feat as an intellectual feat, though it doesn't come to much
—possessed the silly, stupid saxon public with the notion that
the Orangeman is own brother to a Mollymaguire. Well—when
the *United Ireland* people achieve (—and they have contributed
more than any other body of men towards achieving) " Irish "
independence in any sense hostile to the being and the well-being
of Ulster, the world will know the Orangeman for something very
different from the cowardly moonlighters whom we used long ago
in the West of Ireland to call Mollymaguires.—Nor are the
Orangemen of the same kidney with the members of the Ribbon
Society. The truth is—secret association, conspiracy of every
sort, is as repugnant to the mind and character of the North-of-
Irelander as it is congenial to—nay, characteristic of—the mind
and character of the Celt. The Orange Society is a secret society
in no other sense than as any man's own family is a secret society,
as your Cabinet is a secret society, as the London-and-North-
Western Railway Company is a secret society.—Test the Orange
Society by its fruits. Did you ever hear of a murder or other outrage committed by Orangemen on Catholics in the North of
Ireland? Did you ever hear of Catholics being boycotted at
the instigation of the local Orange lodge? The idea is ridiculous !
No ; the Orange Society is—and it is well that you, sir, should
know this—the Orange Society is an army that awaits but the
order *for mobilization*—and when it is *mobilized,* you will see—not

---

[1] What misleads you and saxon statesmen in general is—that you don't *hear*
of this North-of-Irelander. But that is because he doesn't talk. Yes ; and
the Boers didn't talk either. The only sound one heard was the sound—of
their *rifles !* But the rhetoric of a rifle, well aimed, beats *your* rhetoric all to
sticks—" Stone dead has no fellow."—Now the Presbyterian-Scotch-North-
of-Irelander is, *as I knew him,* the nearest approach to the Transvaal Boer
between here and Potschefstroom.

a set of ferocious, yet cowardly devils, whose most daring feat, concocted and contrived *in secret*, is to shoot unarmed and inoffensive men and women—many of these of their own blood and religion,—to maim cattle and destroy property,—but you will see a body of very solid and substantial *men*, who will, in carrying out *their* views of things, stand up in the open field to be shot at —asking for themselves only the right to have some shooting in return !

Now, what think you was the *origin* of this "dangerous" organization—but dangerous *only* to all those who would go about to smash the Empire—a source of comfort and hope to all who wish England well? It was simply the outcome of saxon profligacy during the eighteenth century, as *your* activity has evolved the Irish party in the nineteenth. "Government" would not protect men's lives in the North of Ireland, in districts where the Celtic population preponderated; these men associated for self-defence, and became—the Orange Society. It is, by origin, a defensive, not an offensive Society ; but it can soon be turned to very "offensive" purposes !—Such is the origin and character of the Orange Society. The bulk of Englishmen, and I fear, sir, you among them, don't know anything of these matters. Judged by your acts you don't. —Now I will instruct you a little farther.

The Orange Society has little or no connection with that *other* body of North-Irelanders I have described—namely, the Presbyterian community. *That* body is of the farming class, whereas the Orangemen are, for the greater part, artisans in the towns.[1] The Presbyterian community is "Liberal"—or, till lately, it *was* ; it will now perforce vote Tory ; because you have left no standing-room

---

[1] A battalion of Orangemen could be instantly raised from among the "ship-carpenters" of Messrs. Harland and Wolff in Belfast, with which, sir, if you were a man of war, and *force were a remedy*, you could "go anywhere and do anything."—By the way, the riveters on the Queen's Island tried lately to imitate the saxon "working man" on this side, and got up a strike. They would put in only so many (*far too few*) rivets a day. Idiots ! Do they know the history of ship-building on the Thames ? Do they know the state of the shipping trade at present ? Let them go on in their folly, and they will see the day when the Belfast ship-building firms will place their capital elsewhere ; and the ship-builder's hammer will be heard on the Queen's Island or on Thomson's Bank—no more than at the "*Gobbin Snoot.*"

in the North of Ireland for any but the Celts, and those that won't be put down by the Celts. You have cleared the "flure" for a fine shindy.—The Orangeman, on the other hand, is a Tory. He doesn't like *you*. He believes you are a very mischievous person. He is inaccessible to the winning quality of "good intentions" and "piety." Now, if the Presbyterian farmer and the Orange artisan are not by circumstances forced to combine, Ulster may unwittingly allow the yoke to be placed on its neck. But when Ulster *feels* the yoke, in other words, when the Ulster Presbyterian and the Orangeman *combine* under manifest, acknowledged pressure from without—people of the Celtic and of the saxon "persuasion" would do well to clear off. "I state but the facts."

I have gone into all this explanation because of the impenetrable ignorance of the saxon on all subjects save those which he conceives to have a direct, immediate effect on his bodily comfort. But my line of argument was this: I was showing that, once the Irishry have got all they clamour for, they will find themselves forthwith face to face with *facts*—with two facts, which will—one or both—work their ruin. The first is summed up in the words "*The Ulster Question.*" *That* I have now despatched. Let the Irish party when they sit again in the "Old House" in College Green (—the landlords gone—to Holyhead or to the bottom of the Irish Sea —) and Ireland their own—ask themselves the question—"But Ulster—what shall we do with *it ?*" There is one chance in ten thousand (though I cannot see it) that they will "solve" the Ulster question and stave off reverse *from that quarter.*

ii.—in an Ireland rendered ungovernable—

But they have another enemy who will not be denied ; the blow of that power will equal the blow of the Presbyterian farmer and the Orangeman many times combined ! What is that power? I answer—*the Moral Law of the Universe.* "*No such Law*"—you reply.—Very well. Let us look at *facts*. The "Irish" party in order to put pressure on your Government, resorted to means, or availed itself of means, which, carrying the appearance of success, are only the sure and certain tokens of failure. And now, when the same party think they touch success, they will in reality have to face the *consequences* that invariably follow the use of unjust means. I admit that they were sorely tempted to stoóp to, or at least adopt, these means, because you showed them that by such means you were to be bent and moulded to do what you would *never* otherwise have done. You and England will have your own punishment to bear, and the Irish party can certainly plead that nothing but the means employed would have got them "justice." But to get justice they became *unjust*—and now they will suffer. The means employed by the Irish party were :—

(*a*) To use, or avail themselves of, *crime* as a lever to work on your mind, and gain what they knew they could by this lever make you grant—concessions. I have already shown that it has been a peculiar feature of your statecraft to consider, to cater for, *crime* when your object is to arrive at "true policy"—nay, even when your object is to perform an *act of justice.* Well, you will suffer ; but so will the Irish party. Do they think the crimes they have—I don't say instigated, I don't say approved, but made a lever of— availed themselves of—profited by—do they think these crimes will cease the moment the last shred of English authority disappears in Ireland ? I suppose they do—I suppose it is part of their punishment that they do. Very well, we shall see. But the history of mankind proves that any party which will undertake, whether in consideration of value received (as in this case from you), or for any other reason—that "the same organization which was employed to get up crime shall now be used in suppressing it"—the party that passes, now the word "*no outrages,*" and anon changes that order to "*outrages,*"—that party, I say, as well as the statesman or government that profits by the *mot-d'ordre,* "*no outrage*" to carry through its policy of "concession," and makes up its mind to still bigger "concessions" when the word "*outrages*" is passed along the line—that party and that government are near to richly-deserved destruction.

(*b*) The "Irish" party availed itself of the land-grabbing instinct, so strongly-marked a character in the Irishry, to ruin the landowners. Till this vein was worked the Irish agitation was a hollow affair,—it hung fire miserably. Michael Davitt, a man of genius (in his way) saw what was required ; and Mr. Parnell, though he affirmed that he would not have taken off his coat for anything short of Irish independence—was compelled to join the

(a) from previous fostering of crime.

(b) from previous subversion of the very principle of property.

crusade against the·class to which he himself belonged.   I don't
know, and I don't care whether Mr. Parnell was sincere in his
landowner-*hetze*.   I cannot, from all that I know of him personally,
say whether he perceived that (from the logical and economic
point of view) the principle to which he committed himself was
absolutely rotten, and that *landownership* in one form or other
must exist wherever *civilization* exists.   I cannot tell whether he
does not curse his hypocrisy every time he holds up landowners
(essentially England-loving and order-loving) to the ferocious,
devilish insults of his disorderly horde of Celtic followers, who,
if he flinched, mark me, would assassinate him to-morrow with as
little compunction as Joe Brady (that " grand man," as he was
described by one of his fellow criminals,)[1] drew his knife across
the throat of Lord Frederick Cavendish.   In a word, whatever
Mr. Parnell's opinions may be, and however soon his leadership of the " Irish party " may come to an end,—this much is
certain—that under him, and following his guidance, the Irishry
crossed the boundary line that separates legitimate, even laudable agitation, from agitation that is an offence against the moral
order of the Universe.   Nay, never smile, Parliamentary sir, I
am stating *a fact.*   And I will prove that what I have stated
is a fact, by looking at *results.*—You succumbed to the pressure
put upon you by the doctrine of Michael Davitt as approved and
adopted (1 do not attempt to say how sincerely) by Mr. Parnell.
—And the result ?—Well, to the Irish party, ultimately *ruin*, and
to you, ruin.   Does the " Irish party "—do *you*, sir, really maintain,—*have you the face* to maintain, that in whatever region you
admit the existence of private property, you are not compelled to
admit the existence—nay, the *necessary* existence, of *landownership ?*[2]

[1] What a revelation of the Celtic character at its worst !   A man is described
as *grand;* and his claim to the epithet rests, it seems, *solely* on the evidence
he furnishes *by his acts*, that he is a fiend in human shape.   The Catholic
Church has its work cut out for it when it seeks to restrain such devilry.   Alas,
that Catholicism in Ireland should be made the apologist for, or vindicator of,
such hellish deeds as that of "Skin-the-goat"!

[2] Michael Davitt holds that *the State* ought to let the land.   Very well :
this is a very silly notion ; however, the holder of it isn't bothered with the
eternal *personal* landlord !   He has got rid of him.   But Mr. Parnell and

Meantime, I have only to chronicle the results of this theory. To yourself (though that is not my main point) your acquiescence in Mr. Parnell's views means "indelible disgrace." In 1881, in obedience to the pressure brought to bear by the Davitt-Parnell evangel, you violated contract, broke faith, and in the name of England robbed and beggared thousands of the subjects of Her Majesty. And the end of that transaction will be the abstraction of millions a year from the pocket of the British taxpayer. Is that a result to be desired by a British statesman? There may be no moral laws "of the Universe loafing around"—but you have *"got your fairin'"* [1] at any rate. You are, *somehow*, by accident perhaps,—I say *by design*,—by design of the Almighty, in a cleft stick, and there I leave you. As to the Irish party, for they are in truth my theme at present, they, when they attain separation, will find a landlordless Ireland. Good! But they will find also an Ireland *on the brink of famine.* They have banished the landowners, through your agency. Good! But what becomes of those who were employed, fed, and clothed by the banished landlords? They have, you answer, the land. But you are to levy a land-tax (for you are "landlord now, not king," [2] of Ireland)—a land-tax equivalent to the interest on the money you expend in buying out the landowners. Well, in Irish phrase, I remark: "Don't you wish you may get it?" You will never see a sixpence of the hundred-and-odd millions (more or less) that you expend on expropriating the Irish landowners. Again, you don't seem to see that the destruction of landownership tended to destroy all commerce, all confidence. To understand this let us look at the Irish party sitting in the Old House, and let us ask: what will be their plight?

those who think with him have in fact only substituted one landlord for another—with what result we shall see!—By the way, Michael Davitt's view is in direct opposition to the tendency of the Celt—who desires above all things to own *"a bit of land."*

[1]
> " Ah, Tam, ah, Tam, you'll get your fairin' ;
> In hell they'll roast you like a herrin'."

[2] Which seemed to Shakespeare the last extreme of degradation. (See *Richard II.*, ii. 1.)

The landlords have been brought to their knees. Good. They have been banished. Still better. True : the sitting tenant has the land ; but the sitting tenant *alone* has it, and the would-be occupier is as far as ever from the realization of his hopes. Ireland has not been made as big as France through the banishment of the landowners ; [1] and if it had been made as big, the Celt would soon *squat* the whole of it and cry for more—ultimately, perhaps, cry for the moon,[2]—no matter ; Irish independence is achieved. Hurrah !—But have the landlords gone alone ? No ; they have taken with them some things that did not require even a third-class ticket for the journey to Holyhead. At the same time with the landlords, or rather before them (the process is going on now) *public faith,*[3]—Confidence—has fled, and with confidence Capital ; and with capital and confidence Contract, and the possibility of contract. In a word, sir, while you are arranging terms of surrender in hours-long screeds of English composition, and while the body of clever journalists, lawyers, shopkeepers, adventurers-in-general, and others are applauding you to the echo, while all who, I do not say love England, but who love justice, equity, fair dealing, who recognise roguery when they meet it, and who know what the end of all roguery is,—while these are amazed and confounded—Ireland, the subject of all this composition and these cheers, Ireland, through *your* activity and the activity of those who cheer, is *bleeding to death.*[4] And when

---

[1] Of course I here speak of the landowners who were, in fact, the *English in Ireland.* Landlordism is in the nature of things. To talk of destroying *that,* is to talk of destroying the air. *We* do not commit such folly.

[2] And *his Gladdy,* according to Mr. Sambourne's clever sketch, would, I suppose, do her best to get it for him.

[3] How sarcastic seems the legend on the Bank-of-Ireland notes in the light of recent and current transactions : "*Bona fides reipublicæ stabilitas*" !

[4] I wonder if you are aware that nearly £4,250,000 has been removed from Ireland *within the last year or so*—and that sum from only *ten* leading securities ? If you know this, I wonder whether you think your measures will attract it back again ? I wonder also how you would explain the fact that on the day you were sent for by Her Majesty, Bank-of-Ireland stock fell £7 per share. I could, from personal knowledge, give *startling* proofs of the assertion contained in the text—that Ireland is " bleeding to death." But in regard *to my own experience*—"*satius est silere quam parcius dicere.*" The proofs would cover the space occupied by this entire discourse.

the Irish party becomes the Irish parliament (—or gets itself some-how transmogrified into County Boards,[1] with power to add to its mischief at Westminster—whatever happens it), the Irish party—and you, sir, will have on your hands *a corpse*. And all this has been brought about by attempting to thrust aside the moral laws of the Universe which proclaim that "to find out right with wrong—it may not be." No, sir, no State since the world began, has been built securely on the pillars—the *only* pillars which the Irish party, with your assistance, have set up, namely, Folly, Fraud, and Force.[2] The landowners are avenged.

(*c*) The Irish party, in order to compass its object of attaining liberty—has established a tyranny within the limits of the island which *they hope by this means to set free!* Once more, brilliant sirs, you "find out right with wrong—it may not be." Why, your grand National *League* proves your weakness. It is a huge bubble. It is like one of those monster faces one sees at a pantomime—-frightsome enough, but not really formidable. It can't do any harm, for behind it is only a poor little gutter-boy. I admit this "League" frightens the saxon. But the Irish party ought to have known that the saxon is very easily frightened—in fact that he is subject to periodical fits of fright—at nothing in particular, just as he is subject to periodical and wholly unaccountable and unpredictable fits of the *morals*. To achieve the poor result of frightening him into compliance, the Irish party crossed the boundary-line which

(c) from the previous destruction of the very conditions of social order.

---

[1] But you won't go in for County Boards, even to please the conies among your following. *You dare not.* The Irish party *wouldn't stand it.* And you may always be trusted to make the *most complete* surrender possible.

[2] Here force *is* no remedy, for the good reason that it is exerted *in violation* of the moral laws of the Universe.—Force is, in fact, not the word, rather we ought to call it *violence*. Any statesman may judge of the wisdom or folly—the "justice or injustice"—of a measure by asking : Is there in it the element of *violence?* Shall any honest man in the kingdom find himself by this measure less fit to maintain the struggle for existence? Shall any honest man be *deprived* of one penny? Then if the answer be—*No,*—that will not prove that the measure is a wise one, for there may be other objections ; but if the answer be—*Yes*, then it must not be *so much as named*. It is pernicious and must *fail:* for it introduces *violence*—which is in statesmanship what, according to Carlyle, *hypocrisy* is in human character—"*the one undeniably bad thing.*" Tried by this elementary test of sound statesmanship, what are we to say of your "great "—"just "—"generous "—"healing measures "? But does not the fate of your "measures" prove the truth of the principle?

separates right from wrong, an offence against the moral order of
the Universe that will recoil with crushing force upon the Irish
party itself For what have they done ? To frighten—to " coerce "
England, they have *demoralized* Ireland. They have paid too much,
or rather something far too precious, for their whistle. To terrorize
England they have availed themselves of the only too well-
marked tendency in the Celt towards secret, cowardly combina-
tion ; they have also, having got a nucleus of *willing* conspirators,
acted on the feeble amount of self-reliance in the Celtic character,
and compelled thousands to come in, who would never otherwise
have so much as thought of discontent.—Thus the " League " in-
creases in numbers, and presents a most formidable appearance
with its hundreds of branches—its reports, resolutions, tribunals,
trials, sentences—what not. As towards a strong, worthy England,
it would never be more than the ridiculous monster of the pantomime with a little gutter-boy behind it—it would never develop
anything more formidable than some cowardly offence which could
be dealt with at petty sessions. But the saxon is terrified !   And
the monster becomes more gruesome, for the gutter-boy— astounded
and delighted at his success—makes every possible effort to put
the clown to flight.   He works with might and main all the facial
machinery the monster possesses,—he raises and lowers its eye-
brows, he goggles its eyes, he opens its mouth, he lolls its tongue.
At last the saxon takes to his heels ! Which is all very well.
But there are right ways and wrong ways of attaining an object
which may in itself be quite laudable.   There is no earthly
reason why the Irish should not desire to attain independence.   And God knows there is no great honour in being connected with the England of our time.[1]   But to attain this object,
the Irish party have *killed out* any little manliness, independence, liberty of thought and action, that existed among their
brethren. They will attain their object, but then will come their
punishment.   They will have a community to manage which has
never—never in all its history—given the slightest proof that it could
conduct a rational, just government for one month ; whilst their
way of preparing for governing it has been to degrade the members

---

[1] *A fact which the Colonies will very soon perceive.*

of it to the level of helots.[1]   The assumption is—that such
helots will one of these days be suddenly transformed into grave,
orderly, independent citizens ! and that a parcel of adventurers,
the majority of whom would never have been heard of outside
their own village, and whose sole activity has been devoted to
tripping up a body of legislators consisting, for the greater part,
of blundering saxon clods, that *they* shall become *statesmen,*
and statesmen fit to cope with a case in which the finest
statesmanship—*with its hands clean*—would find all statesmanship useless.   You see the Irish party have committed gross
tactical *blunders* as well as gross moral *wrongs.*   The act of the
Chinaman who burnt down his house in order to get roast pig
was a mere flea-bite in absurdity compared with the act of the
Irish party.   Their act is the act of a man who, wishing to "evict"
or at least drive a tenant out of a house and occupy the house
himself, should very effectually *set fire to the house.*   The tenant
would certainly prefer a mere "*sentence* of death" to the reality
impending every moment.   But where would be the advantage in
ejecting him if, owing to the means that were employed, the house
were burnt to the ground?   The Chinaman had at any rate his
roast pig.   Our ejectors have the charred *site* of the house.   In a
word, the Irish party, in order to set up a government in Ireland,
have resorted to methods which make government impossible.[2]

Summing up then on the Irish party,—when they get Separation
they will be face to face with two grand difficulties, from either,
or both of which, they will receive a crushing blow.   And it
is instructive to note that the evil which they have not them-

---

[1] And that they *could* be degraded to the extent of making *absolute* surrender
of their individual independence proves that they will never attain *national*
independence " as long as wood grows or water runs."

[2] The Home Rule project was never very sound, in all conscience.   In the
the days of Butt, if it seemed chimerical enough, it was at least respectable.   And
the movement in the hands of men like the O'Donoghue and Colonel King-
Harman, the O'Connor Don, Mr. Mitchell Henry, and the Rev. Isaac Nelson
of Belfast, was only to a slight degree mischievous.   But as time has gone on,
and England has become more and more hopelessly inmeshed in the lies of
the Revolution, this movement has taken on several new phases.   " Advance "
has been the watchword.   At last the lowered franchise has evoked the most
extraordinary body of men the world has ever seen—I mean the present Irish
party—not elected by the electors, but *selected* by the despot of the moment.

selves caused is the one evil of the two that *can* be avoided.[1]   But
if they elude or forestall or parry the blow of the one enemy, they
are sure to go down before the blow of the other.   The quarter
from which the first reverse may come is *Ulster.*   When 100,000
Ulstermen (I am now postulating complete Separation) dictate
terms of peace in Dublin Castle, that building will, for the beaten
Celt,[2] assume a significance far more sinister than it possessed in
the days of the dottering saxon *régime,*—when calumnies about its
officials—their inefficiency, tyranny—what not—set afloat by the
enemies of England, were listened to and acted on by the
organization which called itself the Government of England.—
But the Ulsterman may be squared somehow.   The French may
be called in to put him down.   If he is on his day, if he is what
he was not so long ago, he will send the French back sadder, if
not wiser men.   But he may be overpowered by sheer physical
weight of numbers as the 24th was at Isandula.   He then steps
down and out—*as Ulsterman.*   He goes to England, to America
more probably, and the Ulster question is "settled."   I need not
work out the answer any farther.

But the hope of the Irish party that it will ever be able to
construct a government in Ireland will be found as baseless as
the fabric of a vision.   The Celt was never good[3] material to
work upon in establishing civil society, for, as I have said, he ever
tends to barbarism.   But the Irish party have made the problem
absolutely insoluble, for they have availed themselves of the *worst*

---

[1] They will not avoid it, though.   The hatred of the Celt to the "black
North" is such that union between the two sections of Irishmen is, in fact, an
impossibility.   Set free to act, the one *must* exterminate the other.   At present
the Celt has the advantage of the Jacobinism in English government being on
his side.   But the Ulsterman, if he be true to himself and his traditions, *need
not fear.*   Let him work for the *independence of Ulster.*   That is an object
worth his fighting for !

[2] Is it not enough to make any man who loves Ireland curse the brutal
stupidity and profligacy of a Government which, proclaiming "good intentions,"
yet contrives to make possible, nay, to bring us "within measurable distance"
of, the realization of such a thought as this !   And by the way this phrase,
"within measurable distance of civil war" was used in a description of
Ireland when Ireland was an Arcadia to what it is now.

[3] I yield too much here.   The Celt is not, even now, *up to* the level of
constitutional government—any more than our saxon.

qualities of the Celt to produce settled government—which can be produced in any community only by the *best* qualities of the *best* members. He has made murder, outrage, robbery, and tyranny the means of attaining that condition of things which exists but to put down those abominations. He has employed Satan to preach Christ. He has attempted to find out right with wrong—and that *may not be.* He has an Ireland given to him as a punishment—an Ireland where right and the freedom and the very elements of civil government are simply unknown, and where FAMINE will be a constant guest. Liberty is a fine thing ; but in certain contingencies, even high-spirited Irishmen would prefer *food.*—These things are matters of *demonstration.*

Let us now take our bearings, and then proceed. I was invoicing the particulars to which your activity in this matter of dealing with the Irish question differed from that of your predecessors. And my *last* remark was, that you *created* the party *at whose bidding* you have brought England to the present pass. This Irish party has in it nothing intrinsically formidable. It is in itself a sorry sham. But if an ignorant clown runs away from a bogey, he may fall down a precipice and break his absurd neck as effectually as if he fled from the very devil himself. The fear is groundless, but the result of the fear is very real. That is your position. And when you stand up to make your proposals, you will do so, not induced thereto by any spontaneous conviction arising in your own mind from knowledge and *experience* of the subject you are about to legislate upon—but in panic terror at the all-frightsome contortions produced on that monster face by that poor little gutter-boy ! This is God's truth. And when one reflects that that face is of *your own devising*—the eyes that goggle, the mouth that opens, and the tongue that lolls—and that the gutter boy is of your own *rearing*, that you are the nurse in whose arms he did his mewling and his puking, the whole thing is perilously near the region of the ridiculous—and would instantly lead all persons who *know* the matter to explode in laughter were it not that they are restrained by the thought that there is at stake—the fate of an empire.

'But it was you who gave the hideous sham all its hideous being.

Having now taken our bearings—having examined the peculiarities of your activity, I pass on to glance at your actual measures, those " generous " measures, to which you were moved

F

by the gutter-boy of your own creation, working a monster visage
of your own design. It is true that you might prefer these
former measures to pass quietly into the region of "ancient
history ; " but I have to do for them what has not yet been done,
no, not by all the brilliant leading articles of ever so many able
editors.[1]   I have to examine them in the light of the moral laws
of the Universe.   In these laws you may possibly believe, when
you are driven back, your choice battalions shattered to atoms,
your positions carried, your standards captured, and the only
possible command that can pass your lips, that command of
despair :—" *Sauve qui peut !* "—you may in that awful moment
perhaps—or when you can collect your thoughts—be given the
power to see and acknowledge that in very deed there *are* Moral
Laws in the Universe—Laws which were, I do not say as *active*,
(for *that* they have been since the evolution of man, nay, long
before,) but as well ascertained, as well established, and as clearly
recognised by us (though not by you) to be *absolute* in their sanctions, when you first touched the Irish Question as they are now.[2]

It was you, the guardian of society, who gave effect to out-rage—the Clerkenwell explosion and its train—the work of the enemies of society, y legislative outrage com-mitted pari passu in measures of spoliation against ociety itself.   In order to make the Irish Difficulty ancient history, you
came forward—late in the Sixties of the century—with a
Trinity-in-Unity of " measures "—a Trinity-in-Unity as " incompre-
hensible," I assure you, to all who understand the Difficulty by
actual contact with it as that Trinity so definitely and graphically
described in the Creed " called of St. Athanasius."   You *took in*
the Irish Difficulty. In the language of Mr. Toole, you " saw it at
a glance."   *Glance* is the word—I don't care how many days and
nights you spent on the operation. If you had brought the
proper *mental and moral* faculties to bear on the work, you
would long ago have chucked this wretched, this miserable,
this contemptible " Question " overboard ; you would have

---

[1] *Vide* Appendix, Note C.

[2] Your activity and its result will to all time be cited as proof of the existence of those moral laws.   And that is one reason why I wish to discuss your
measures—to show, namely, a distant posterity that the laws were ascertained
at a time when *to all appearance* they had not been ascertained, or when the
knowledge of them, though ascertained by former investigators, had been
lost.   For, really, in most of your political activity we have to lament not
so much the absence of statesmanship, as of common *honesty*.

initiated a policy that was in strict conformity with the Moral
Laws of the Universe ;—and having done so, you could have
possessed your soul in patience, no matter what befell ("*im-
pavidum ferient ruinae* " !) — and looked forward to the day when
the Irish Difficulty—obsolete, not merely as the Heptarchy, but
as the trials of Lamech—would decorously date itself at a period
if not so distant, yet as irrevocably *past* as "the years beyond the
flood." But you and the saxon would have something sensational.
You wanted "heroic" legislation, and the saxon—who admires
what he doesn't understand—gave you the chance. Now, let us
look at your measures and their results. Let us go back in
thought to the later Sixties of the century. Let us look at your
Trinity of measures.

The struggle between the Northern and Southern States of
America, which ended in 1864, left stranded a number of Irish
adventurers who had taken part in it. The war over, their occu-
pation was gone. They then turned their attention to a "settlement " of the Irish question. But there was nothing terrible about
them. A sergeant's guard at the beginning and the hangman at
the end could have "settled " for *them.* Now,—one bit of their
"devilment " was an attempt to blow in the wall of Clerkenwell
prison, in which some of their brother " Fenians " were incar-
cerated. The only result was that some persons passing at the
time lost their lives. The prisoners were not set free. Now you
were ranging well up towards office just then, and wanted a
policy. Will it be believed by posterity that the Clerkenwell
explosion furnished you with a policy ? I don't profess to see
the connection between the outrage and your policy. And I
should never have imagined that such a connection existed, had
you not yourself given public assurance of the fact. You gave
such assurance,—nay, you did more : you even indicated the
particular measure which that outrage suggested to your mind
and which it thus brought *within the region of practical politics.*
It suggested to you the necessity of *ruining the Church Establishment in Ireland.* I don't know, and never have been able
to *imagine* how the outrage *could* suggest the destruction of
the Irish Church. I should have thought there was about

F 2

as much connection between the two things as between the
Goodwin Sands and the building of Tenterden steeple.—Were
you convinced by the outrage that the Irish Establishment must
be very immoral in its teaching and ought to be abated as a
nuisance, seeing that its members could be guilty of such a
diabolical outrage? But, sir, the perpetrators of the crime were
American-Irish Catholics ; and the Irish Establishment was *Protestant.* The miscreants had really very little to do with Ireland,
and nothing at all to do with the Established Church.[1] The
bishops and clergy of the Province of Canterbury are surely not
responsible for polygamy in Utah? Or, ascertaining that the
perpetrators of the outrage were Catholics and having a hazy
notion that the Irish Establishment was *Catholic* (as, *e.g.,* the
Scottish Establishment is Presbyterian), did you determine to
destroy it for producing such scoundrels as those who committed
the Clerkenwell outrage? But, as I have already told you, the Irish
Establishment was *Protestant.* But even had it been Catholic,
you were rather wide of the mark. It is true that the Fenians were
Catholics—if anything ; it is true, also, that they were of Irish ex-
traction. But it would have been very unjust towards the Catholic
Church in Ireland to visit on it the sins of a set of cowardly ruffians
whose *ancestors* were Irish Catholics, but who themselves really
acknowledged the authority of no Church, Catholic or Protestant.[2]
Or, again, did the Clerkenwell explosion suggest " Disestablish-
ment " merely in the way of analogy : I mean, did you conceive
the idea of blowing sky-high the Irish Establishment as the Fenians
thought to blow up Clerkenwell Prison ? " These fellows," you
may have cried, " have blown up something, and I want to blow
up something—*I will blow up the Irish Establishment !* " Or,
lastly, was it a case of quailing before what is, or even what only
seems to be, *determination to win* on the part of an opponent—a
fear to stand up and fight your corner—is it anything like the

[1] The Fenians as a body did not merit the reproach of being righteous
over-much. They were *not* gospel-greedy.

[2] You must surely at an early stage of your progress have been made aware
of the fact that the Irish Establishment was Protestant ; but it may have been
then too late to hold your hand. However, the way you "went for " the Vatican
soon afterwards would seem to favour the guess I have ventured in the
text.

craven cowardice that makes the saxon Government run away, not merely before the rifle-practice of the Africanders, but also before the gogglings and grimaces of the "National League"?[1]

Some of these theories may appear very stupid ; but I am once more in the presence of *mystery.*   And I am very stupid at solving riddles of any sort : *Davus sum.*   You have vouchsafed to assert that *the Clerkenwell explosion brought the destruction of the Irish Church within the domain of practical politics*, yet neither you nor any of your "followers" have ever—so far as I know—added a *Targum*—you have never by gloss, scholium, or explanation of any kind shown the connection that existed in your mind between the Clerkenwell explosion and the destruction of the Irish Church.   But we have your word *for the fact.*

I now proceed to occupy firmer ground.   That Clerkenwell explosion and its result furnish a key, an explanation in a nutshell, of your entire political activity, not only in the Irish question, but in your foreign policy as well.   With your foreign policy, however, I have nothing *at present* to do.   Let us now examine for a short space this Clerkenwell explosion as a suggester of a policy—and in it we shall find the elements *of all your political activity.*   This will materially shorten our labours in examining your other "measures."

1. The explosion was, in a sense, an *accident :* if the explosion caused the policy, it is fair to argue that if the accident had not happened you would not have arrived at the policy—unless, of course, some other suitable accident had happened.   Now suppose the Irish Church was a *real grievance*, what are we to think of the statesman whose activity in removing it depended on an *accident ?*[2]   But, as was your policy in that case, so has your policy

---

[1] And really the Transvaal affair was never very formidable, save to a Government determined above all things to avoid the sin of "blood-guiltiness."   But I should be easier in my mind if Government had some *à priori* method of learning high humanitarian doctrines—instead of requiring such experience as was afforded by the actions at Laing's Nek, the Ingogo River, and Majuba Hill—to convince them of truths which (*if they were truths*) might have been attained long before, one would have thought, by the mere ordinary working of the *conscience.*

[2] Suppose the Fenians, even though "trusting in God," had neglected to "*keep their powder dry*," and that the explosion had not come off,—then,

been in every case ; it depends on the wind, or a jogging of your elbow. Every "measure" is the result of what is essentially an *accident.*

2. The Clerkenwell explosion was an *outrage.* And every step you have taken in your Irish policy has been taken at the bidding of *outrage*—and again *outrage*, and ever *outrage.*

3. The Clerkenwell explosion and your policy had *no rational connection.* Pardon me for saying so : you have asserted that there *was* a connection—the connection of cause and effect. But I speak here of *rational connection—such* a connection did not exist. If you had been moved by the explosion to wear Shakespeare collars, and said so, we should have taken your word ; but you surely don't maintain that the logical faculties of mankind would enable anybody to follow and acquiesce in your reasoning, and say, "Of course ; when an explosion of this sort takes place, what is to be done? One must, of course, wear Shakespeare collars." [1] In other words, your policy was—as towards the Clerkenwell explosion—an *irrelevancy.* So has every bit of policy been which you have adopted on this Irish question.

4. Lastly, a policy of irrelevancy, suggested by an accident, and enforced by outrage, naturally *failed.*—And the destruction of the Irish Church—so far from *settling* the Irish question—rendered the solution of it for ever more difficult.

Such was your first trinity of measures :— Let us now glance at your measures. They were three in number. I have called them a Trinity-in-Unity, because you insisted they must all go together.

(i.) your Irish Church Act, 1. The Establishment was to be destroyed—the Upas-tree cut down. You cut it down. Were you aware, I wonder (I am sure

failing some other "suitable" *accident* (we have had lately three or four first-class explosions in London : and there was, to be sure, the earthquake in Java)—the Irish Establishment might be in existence at the present moment. But in that case, what becomes of the *Upas-tree* theory? If the Irish Church was a Upas-tree, it ought to have been removed, even without the (to you) very directly suggestive force of the Clerkenwell explosion.

[1] I hope you don't think me tedious. You see I pay you the compliment of weighing your words (as I hope you—in your position of responsible statesman—weighed them). If I have found them "wanting," is that wholly my fault?

your saxon following were not aware), that *not one penny*[1] went
into the pockets of the Catholic Irish from your operations on the
Upas-tree ?   You plundered the Church, but the Irishry got none
of the swag.   True, a system of intermediate " education " was
afterwards established out of part of the plunder ; and that system
is rapidly making true education a bit of "ancient history" in
Ireland.

2. You plundered the landowners by giving to the tenants the (ii.) your
" *right* " of sale, that is to sell to anybody they pleased, that which Land Act
by contract belonged to the landowners (—save in a certain part of of '70,
Ireland where the tenants and landowners had come to an understanding on the point—where, in other words, the right of sale
did *not* involve breach of contract).

3. You introduced a University Education Bill—which involved (iii.) your
spoliation—but I needn't dwell upon it : the Irish party—even at University
this early period formidable—turned you out of office because Education
your measure did not go far enough.   I think you learned then Bill.
that you ought always to ascertain what will satisfy the Irish party,
and to offer no less ; for they will take no less.

Such then, in short, was your policy in the early Seventies,—and
the result ?   *Failure.*   But how could it be otherwise?   You
were what is called in French politics an Opportunist—a mere
political Micawber, " waiting for something to turn up."   You
were—in the presence of, let us say, glaring injustice, abominable
wrong-doing—as immovable as the Rock of Cashel.   But when
you were driven to action by the enemies of England, *then*—you
acted. " After all, " why dwell on your first set of measures?   There
is no reason for doing so, save, indeed, this :—that all your after-
policies were more stark-nakedly absurd, and were therefore more
transient in their (apparently) good effects, and more permanently
disastrous in their bad effects.   In these evil respects they leave
all other measures known to history far behind.

---

[1] Before 1833 the tenants would have got back a *small portion* of their tithe :
that was all.   As the case stood—the tithes having been paid by the landlords
—the tenants got literally *nothing*.   If the ferocious Catholic Celts could have
seen the Protestant Churches demolished, could have danced on their ruins,
that would have been something !   But then the Protestant Churches stand to
the present hour !

Such, too,
were :—

Pass on over ten years, ten years in which these "beneficent" measures had time to show their beneficence, and what do we find? That the Irish Question has moved towards solution one inch? Not so. The Irish Question is once more a blazing topic—for you have once more come up into office—come up smiling—to settle the Irish Question.[1] Premising that during the '70 period and this

---

[1] Your political opponents say that your sole desire is—not *primarily* to settle any question—though, of course, you don't wish to fail—but *to get and keep office*—in the sense that for instance at the present time you would be ready to modify your proposals if, by doing so, you could "keep the Cabinet together," —which means, of course, *hold office*. But if this be so, how can you talk of introducing "just," "generous" measures for Ireland? Why take the name of *Justice* in vain? If any proposal is modified in the slightest jot or tittle to keep the Cabinet together—then the whole policy is a bit of damnable hypocrisy. It is a very long time since the light of nature enabled men to arrive at the formula—based on their observation of acts and their consequences : "*Fiat Justitia, ruat cœlum.*" The Christian-philanthropical-French-Revolution version of the maxim seems to be :—When, led by desire to obtain or hold office, you introduce, at the bidding of victorious Rebellion (victorious through former acts of your own), a measure of farther surrender,—exercise your ingenuity to find out a policy that will satisfy Rebellion and yet not offend the consciences of colleagues. It does not look well to see the leading men in the Government dropping off. But if they *will* resign, you can put a set of figure-dummies in their place, and the saxons in Parliament and out of doors will never know the difference! You must above all things avoid offending the party of Rebellion, for they are your masters, and can inflict upon you the only punishment you acknowledge, namely, loss of office. Having now got a "workable measure"—*i.e.* one that will satisfy Rebellion and not explode the Cabinet (all explodable material having, indeed, removed itself), you appoint a day for your statement—for the opening of one of the seals in your Revelation. What excitement! What expectation! Several saxons have been from early morning in their places ; and their object? *to hear the Orator make* "*his most brilliant effort*" (English composition of a certain sort has a fascination for the saxon)—and several "working men" have knocked off for the half-day (a very congenial operation : but how about their families ?) to *cheer* the Orator as he goes down to the House. Well, at last he rises and goes through his composition. And the *substance* of it all is—the "workable measure" I have just described,—the origin of the whole wretched thing being a determination—come what may—to retain power! Yet this "workable measure" would be called by the Orator and his faithful and high-souled saxon myrmidons *an act of justice*. But, good God, sir, what has *Justice* to do with this matter? Why should this particular virtue be mentioned any more than Faith, Hope, Charity, or early rising? "*Astræa*" is not "*Redux*" when such a measure passes. Nay, as respects all concerned in the transaction—(save, indeed, those who retired from the Cabinet) *Justice* is as far from them and

second spell of activity the "idea" was daily gaining ground (a natural result of your first Land Act) that the *land belongs to the Tenant* [a form of Lie 8, p. 15]—I go on with my cataloguing.

1. You introduced a Bill to compel the landowner to give "compensation" to a tenant whom he removed under the terms of the contract made between them.   He might require the land for the purpose of letting it out in building-sites—for, in short, a hundred beneficial objects—but see how injustice here tends to force the community back to barbarism.   The sitting tenant, though such a thing was excluded by the very terms of the contract, could claim from the landowner *compensation for disturbance !*   The very word *disturbance* carries with it the suggestion that the landowner, in putting an end to a contract, in accordance with its terms, a contract which the tenant entered into with his eyes open, and which he could end on the same terms—inflicts a *wrong* on the tenant !   It seems as if we were become judicially blind as to what is justice and what is injustice.   We call an act *unjust* that has not a particle of injustice about it : on the other hand, acts that reek of injustice we call *acts of justice !* as if justice were the very quintessence of them !

(i.) your "Disturbance" Bill.

This measure was rejected by the Lords.   And quite characteristically its rejection by the Lords was made the occasion of a cry against their House—some liars going so far as to trace all the outrages, &c. (which grow in Ireland as naturally as the shamrock), to its rejection !   Of course, this was a very fair point for

their act as if she inhabited the great nebula in Orion.   There is, indeed, a thing called Justice—and in public or private life you act contrary to her behests *at your peril*.   But she has nothing to do with *this* galley.—Since writing this note I hear that the amount of compensation to be given to the landlords on their *violent* expropriation and banishment will be only *half* the sum mentioned at first.   It is thus hoped that the "great measure" will have a better chance of becoming "law."   Very well.   But why talk of *Justice* in such a connection?   The claims of Justice don't shift with the interests of one certain statesman.   Justice to the Irish landowners is unchangeable as the foundations of the Universe, and Justice will—in the end—be amply vindicated.   The truth is—Government in this country is a predatory organization.   Now if, in any nefarious project of plunder, " Ministers' " only anxiety is *to keep together*, how, I want to know, can they take into their mouths the sacred name of *Justice ?*

the Irish party : it was *their game.* As a matter of fact the Lords could have been got to swallow the measure—as is proved by their swallowing, after making the decent number of wry faces, a much more pernicious measure—if there be any degrees in what is in itself, first midst and last, rank injustice and tyranny.[1]

(ii.) your
Land Act of
'81,

2. Then in 1881, came the last, positively the last, "great "healing" measure for Ireland. And why the last? Because it was—don't you see?—to "settle" the Irish question. There was to be no more trouble in Ireland. St. Patrick *resurgent* in *you,* sir, was to banish from Erin the toads and serpents of anarchy, crime, and poverty. Look at the leading articles of the time, columns on columns—in fact, whole parasangs—of newspaper matter all in this sense. See the cartoons in the "comic" journals, &c. The Saturnian age was to *return* to Ireland—having never, by the way, existed in that island ; "Astræa" was to be "Redux" this time, and no mistake, and why? *"Justice was to be our guide !"* —and she couldn't be our guide without having been brought back. Now here again comes up mystery, and we will avoid it, merely observing that no human being removed by one degree from the flint-implement stage of moral development (—of course the majority among us are only at that stage, if so far advanced,) but would be by that "measure" offended against the wind a mile.—But this talk of *injustice* grows monotonous ; *every one* of the measures introduced by your successive Govern-ments[2] for the solution of the Irish question is, I do not say

---

[1] If the Lords had allowed their House to be smashed to pieces rather than pass your Land Bill of 1881, what a strong position they would now occupy in the opinion of the non-saxon portion of the people of England ! They would, in fact, have saved Ireland to the Empire and prevented an incalculable amount of personal loss and misery. But the saxon element was too strong in their House and out of it.

[2] Or rather *by you.* Your *Governments* have very little to say in devising any of your great measures. You are the Achilles, whose wrath (rather, whose activity) is to cause numberless woes to his countrymen. A more contemptible set of ciphers than your present Myrmidons never sat on the Ministerial bench. *Extinct* volcanoes forsooth ! These never in their whole lives could rise to the dignity of a visible eruption ! Mere *sham* volcanoes. Your Chancellor of the Exchequer is indeed a volcano of a sort.—He is a "mud-volcano." With all his violence of manner, how weak he is ! Always

unjust in some of its provisions, but *compact* of injustice— injustice in warp and woof—injustice in the body and soul of it —its *essence* injustice.—I now pass on to glance at your grand Land Act from the point of view of *practical* economics (saxons will please observe that I use the word *practical* here[1]) and intellectual consistency.

The Irishry were not yet happy. They had started a Land League, the object of which was to abolish *rack*-rents, that is, *all* rents. I have before intimated that *rack*-rents are a theoretical and "practical" absurdity. Any rent is a rack-rent—that I don't want to pay. And I can live in such a style as to make a rent of five shillings a year for Chatsworth a rack-rent.—But I don't now wish to dwell on such points. You, sir, believe (though it is hard to say what you believe—or rather, what you will believe this day week,—some outrage in Ireland may bring you up with a "great measure" condemning us all to Christy-Minstrel collars), I say, *you* believe there are such things as rack-rents—or did in 1881. *I* say you "went for" a phantom. If you went for a reality, let us see exactly what you did, and what the result was.

Ireland being rack-rented, you were determined to "put down" rack-rents. To do this, you introduced a measure which, like *all* your great measures, was simply such a mass of involved and complicated *details* (see p. 3) that your audience received from your speech what Mr. Goschen would probably call a *staggerer ;* [2] your *great* effort had thrown people into the condition of not knowing whether they stood on their heads or their heels : the bearings of things had got all awry. Men like Mr. Gibson and Mr. Plunket, who know something about *part* of Ireland, discussed the

the advocate of a policy designed by somebody else—a mere elephantine *Scholiast.*

[1] Saxons will not "observe" this nor very much else in the present monograph. To begin at the beginning and read on to the end—to weigh and consider (as Bacon recommends)—what is here set down, to agree or disagree, *but always with a reason*—this would prove you to be, in *my* sense, *no saxon,* though you could trace your strain on both sides of the house to the loins of Aethelwulf.

[2] I beg pardon. I think that this admirable word is confined—in classical usage—to *moral* delinquencies of a particularly heinous and startling character —as, *e.g.*, certain statements in the *Financial Reform Almanac.*—Mr. Goschen will correct me if I am wrong.

Bill as a Bill (if I remember right—but I may be wrong),—the poor craven saxon said never a word. And reason good. The saxon, in the presence of any complicated problem or complicated statement (and he may trust you, sir, to make, by a complicated statement, a complicated problem infinitely more complicated)—I say the saxon is as incapable of keeping his small wits in such a presence—as Sir Pertinax Macsycophant was unable "to keep his back straight *in the presence o' a great mon.*" [1]

The "great" Land Bill of 1881 was a good specimen of your matured manner Detail, fogging detail, bewildering detail [2]—which deceived not only the saxons, but would have deceived "the very elect," if any such persons had been found on either side of the House; this was *the* feature of the measure. It fogged the intellect, but it didn't fog the moral sense. *The very first clause* of your measure implied *robbery ;* why, then, didn't somebody get up after your speech and move [3]—and take a division on the motion—that the Bill should be read a second time that day six months ?—This may not be Parliamentary *form,* I know. But this is *what ought to have been done.*—I must add that the essential elements of your 1881 Bill were (as I have before observed) those which you pronounced at the era of your first Land Act to involve *spoliation.* But "many things had happened" since 1870. Well, as liars ought to have long memories, so he that proposes a measure founded on dishonesty would

[1] Sir Pertinax seems to have given up the attempt very early in life ; our saxon seems to have been *always* incapable of *making* it.

[2] It was said at the time that only three men in the House ever really mastered the details of that Bill. I know Mr. Healy was one, and I think you were, yourself, one of the two others. I forget the third. I hope History has her eye upon him.

[3] The mistake made by those who *ought,* one would think, to see the wickedness of your "just," &c., measures is—that they, for one moment, *entertain them—discuss them.* When you introduce your new measures—somebody ought, *at once,* to propose *their rejection.* What *Justice,* if she were *our guide,* would demand is—that some properly authorised officials should take your impending Bills (after your speeches on them) and, together or severally, *kick* them from the table to the door of the House. When the wretched misbegettings were fairly *outside,* Justice would *smile*—a thing she has not, to my certain knowledge, done for these many years—in connection with English legislation.

need to be very ingenious in arranging the structure so as not to demonstrate its weakness before the eyes of even a saxon Parliament; and you are very ingenious. You went for the three F's—that is, you went for a project which you had, by anticipation, criticized as *spoliation*. Fair Rents and the general working of the Act were to be shunted on to a *Commission*. I wonder what blundering and profligate statesmanship would do without Commissions! So, a set of adventurers—farmers, shop-keepers, briefless barristers, with a sprinkling of men of some standing to give the appearance of respectability [1]—these, I say, went roaming over Ireland "fixing fair rents." Of course, the whole activity of these landloupers was directed towards robbing with the *appearance* of justice! In any healthy com-munity, where the notions of property were what they ought to be —but where police and settled government were not as yet intro-duced (as, *e.g.*, on the banks of the Stanislow), the landowner— when these "Commissioners" came loafing around, spying his land, smelling the end of their walking sticks, and then affixing the "fair" rent [2]—would probably get excited,—*shooting* might be the word,—in which case the intruders would be lucky if they were allowed to sheer off without carrying each a brace of bullets in his hull. And the landowner would be quite within his right. There being no settled government, he must protect himself. Under a settled and just government the police would protect

[1] And a sprinkling of Conservatives to give the appearance of impartiality. But the best record for any man who aspired to become a Land-Commis-sioner was—to have stumped the country for "Mr. Gladstone" before the elections of 1880. By the way, you don't seem to have insisted on your *sub*-Commissioners (at any rate) being able to speak, write, and spell the English language "with propriety."—When one is robbed, one likes to be robbed by a man who has, by his manner, &c., "robbed" thievery of half its—objectionableness.

[2] A Fair Rent, good sir, is what a man can get for the use of land or house in open market. The rent couldn't be more than that sum, and it oughtn't to be less. This principle you act upon every day of your life. Yet you have used all the brute force of the ever-hateful saxon Government to set aside the principle—or rather to trample it underfoot, in one whole division of the triple Kingdom. That is, only *within a limited area*, do you say? But you cannot limit the area ; and you will soon (for the demoralization is spreading rapidly) have to give your days and nights to a Land Bill for *England*. Can it be that there *is* a God, after all?

him ; under *your* government the police held him down while
your Commissioners robbed him.

The Land Act, then, was a big iniquity; but it was also a big
insanity, a big humbug, and a costly humbug. It cost about
£100,000 a year; and its results were—I don't say *nil*,—we
might all be thankful if it had been merely a dead letter—but
such as to *abolish* peace and progress in Ireland for *our* time.[1]

Let us look at the *folly* of the measure. You give, it seems,
days and nights to devising schemes for your country's welfare.[2]
Now, will you permit me to ask you whether the following obvious
deductions did not occur to your mind when, for the sake of peace
and order—or office, you thought of going for the three F's :—

1. That as your bogus-tribunals lowered rents, the tenant-right
(—a "right" which you had before created in the greater part
of Ireland by robbery of the landowners) would become *pari
passu* more valuable.

2. That the land-hunger, which not even the terrors of the
Land League and the National League have succeeded in
restraining,[3] must drive the would-be tenant to the money-lender
—bank—what not,—and in the South and West, to the *gombeen*-
man.

3. That, therefore, your grand legislation could—in the very

---

[1] Now, sir, this is not rhetoric; this is *fact*. And peace and progress
will never return to Ireland till such measures as your great Land Act are
regarded as the result of devilish, traitorous malice, or stark-naked *lunacy*.
When they are so regarded, *and therefore avoided*, peace and progress will be
at least *possible*. But that won't be in your day or mine. The fires lighted by
the French Revolution—*cleansing* fires they will prove themselves in the end—
have yet much offal to burn up in "civilized" society. Those fires may *con-
sume* our whole "Christian" civilization, but all will be well *in the end*. The
community which could receive with applause, and help you to carry out, this
nefarious scheme of robbery—that community, I say, is fit fuel for those
cleansing fires, and, at any risk, *it must have them*.

[2] I wish you would take Dr. Johnson's advice and "give your days and nights
to the volumes of Addison." You might, by so doing, attain, even at your time
of life, "a style familiar but not coarse, and elegant but not ostentatious"—and
(I may add with true Johnsonian antithesis) clear but not nebulous, and terse
though not wordy ; besides (which is more to the point), all honest men in
the three kingdoms would *breathe freely*.

[3] Witness their constant (*and they must be constant*) denunciations of "land-
grabbing."

nature of things—benefit only the actual (or "sitting") tenant ;
for if the actual tenant chose to sell his farm after having secured
a *judicial rent* (*risum teneatis, amici ?*), the incoming tenant would
have to pay for the land *in interest* on the money borrowed from
the bank or *gombeen*-man, and in "fixed, fair" rent to the landowner a yearly sum equal to or even higher than the original
rent—that is, the rent as it stood before your bog-trotters began
their operations. This was the obvious truth which Mr.
Goschen called (and did well to call) attention to, when he was
met by a saxon howl of denial !—and by that immortal Barclay's
"*staggering*" rejoinder that the choice was between this arrangement and *rack*-rents ! To which I reply, that what this *vir
ornatissimus et honestissimus*—this Barclay, to wit—calls "*rack-
rents*" are infinitely preferable to the arrangement in the Crofters'
Bill (another *insane iniquity*) which enjoyed the privilege of his
championship.

4. That the assumption by the State of the function of settling
tariffs—a thing long since abandoned as *impossible*—would lead
to ugly complications,—in fact, to economic and social anarchy.

5. That these considerations proved the (imagined) measure
to be, in every sense, a *rotten* measure—rotten, as judged by
the intellect ; rotten, as judged by the moral sense ; and
therefore—

6. That in God's name you must abandon it—must never think
of it again, must leave the Question insoluble were you to live a
thousand years, rather than try to solve it by such a measure.

Well, unfortunately for yourself and for England, you did not
knock against these considerations in preparing your "great
measure" ; and you did not abandon it. You launched it, and
(this is almost inconceivable !) you must have at least *hoped* that
it would succeed. That it did not succeed is proved by the
fact that—notwithstanding your assurances to the contrary—*it
has made Ireland a wilderness*,[1]—and also,—a thing that will

---

[1] You *somehow* brought yourself to affirm that by your Land Act the landowners would *really lose nothing !* And that mischievously feeble personality,
Lord Carlingford, explained that the landlords, when they had their rents
fixed by the Land Courts, would be certain of getting them, because they
would in demanding them be supported by Government ! Really, the English

come home to you—that you are again on the war-trail after the
Irish Difficulty! And so you will be, sir, as long as you breathe
the vital air, and occupy the position of Prime Minister. Your
efforts in 1881 were futile—save in making the Difficulty all
but insurmountable now to the ablest statesman in the universe
—and *quite* insurmountable to you.

(iii.) your
Arrears Act,

3. Following up your great Land Act as a sort of appendix
came the *Arrears* Act, whereby, *e.g.*, a scoundrel-tenant could—by
swearing a few lies—the easiest thing in life on the other side of
St. George's Channel—*fine* his landlord for being so tolerant
and patient as to let him run into arrears in his rent—through
bad seasons or any other cause; while the *honest* tenant who,
under the same circumstances, made an effort and paid his rent,
had an opportunity to curse his folly, when he saw his dishonest
neighbour, with his tongue in his cheek, *lodge his money in the
bank*, and yet get his arrears paid for him! Comment is needless.[1]

(iv.) your
Labourers'
Act,

4. Then came the Labourers' Act, by which, if you, down at
Hawarden, for example, were surrounded by a population that
was artificially—by governmental agency in fact—incensed against
you, made to believe that you were an intruder and a robber (and
so, indeed, even *you*—you, the "great" humanitarian statesman
—would have been regarded, had you lived in Ireland any time
these last five years *as a landowner*)—that population, under
your Labourers' Act, would be able to conduct an exterminating
war against you,"*without handling a gun.*" The "local authority"—

language, strong as it is in denunciatory expressions, altogether fails one in
the presence of such villany! Is, then, an eviction *not* a sentence of death
when the tenant refuses to pay the "judicial" rent without forty per cent.
abatement? And would Mr. Morley of the carpet-bag *always* approve of
Her Majesty's forces being employed to evict tenants who had got their rents
"fixed"—and then "could" not pay without forty per cent. abatement? By the
by, a Professorial person on the Land Commission (one Baldwin, if I remember
rightly) obliged the world with a definition of *fair rent*. A fair rent was
a rent such as the actual individual tenant—the tenant in court—could pay,
"*and still live comfortably*"!!

[1] I will only ask whether any expressions I have used or *can* use in regard
to the doings of your Government in Ireland are, or could be, too strongly
denunciatory. Stupidity, injustice, insolence, hypocrisy—these are its ever-
present hall-marks.—And yet you are *again* selected to "settle" the Difficulty!

consisting of the bitter foes of your race and religion—would inform
you that a certain plot of ground was required by the said "local
authority" for the purpose of erecting on it labourers' cottages. You
might protest that you did not want any additional labourers on your
farm (I am now speaking of an actual case within my own knowledge)—that you had labourers' cottages—all that you wanted—
elsewhere on your property. In vain. The "local authority"
would take the land, make a beginning by erecting one cottage ;
and then two labourers would contend, in your presence, as to
which should be accepted as your tenant, and one would threaten
point-blank that if you didn't take *him*, he *would do for you !* This
is the sort of government that you have established in Ireland; and
by this and such acts you have made Ireland what I have already
called it—a very hell to live in.—I need not add that the sole
object of erecting the cottages was to lay siege to the unfortunate
gentleman who holds the land, and to force him to clear out.[1]—
Such, sir, is the legislation by which you hope—or *say* you hope—
to settle the Irish Question.

5. But your legislative activity was not yet at an end. You
had constituted yourself the champion of the being I have called
the "saxon" in our English community—of the element within our
own borders that makes for our destruction—of the parasite which,
in ever-increasing numbers and power, threatens England with
bankruptcy, famine, extinction. Him—this saxon—you nursed
into dangerous life by many measures—notably by your Ballot
Act and your "Education" Act. In short, you placed him in
the fair way of reducing England to the condition of a corpse.
What you did for the Celt—our greatest danger outside our own
borders—I have already recounted. But this drama of degradation was not yet complete. Your artistic sense perceived that
something was wanting. The saxon and the Celt must be made
to join hand in hand for our destruction ! This consummation of

*(v.) your
Franchise
Act.*

[1] There was no sort of objection to him personally—nor in the case of
99 per cent. of the landowners that have been banished. They represented
England : that was enough. And because the Celt raises a howl against them
—egged on to do so by the caitiff saxon government—that government next
proceeds—having first robbed them—to banish them ! And all in the name
of *Justice !*

G

all your activity you brought about by your Franchise Act of
1885.

By this Act the destinies of the British Empire were committed
to the keeping of *the lowest of the people ;* and that arrangement has never succeeded since the world began.   Mark : that
Act might with more propriety be called a *disfranchising* Act, for
its main effect was to *deprive* of the franchise the classes who had
hitherto possessed it, and who, from the very nature of the case,
had divers interests, and to hand it over to the class which, on
points affecting its interests, *as it understands them,* will always *vote
solid ;* for *its interests* are limited to considerations regarding its own
back and its own stomach.   In other words, you committed the
government of England and the Empire to the " saxon "—to the
class which swarms with saxons.   To effect this, you knocked to
pieces the English Constitution—that Constitution, the foundation
of which was laid by those men—noble in nature and act, as they
were noble in station—who won the Great Charter of 1215.—Of
course, you would not have been allowed to commit such an offence
against the rights of Englishmen (for the Constitution means, or
meant, nothing more nor less than a set of well-ascertained *rights*),
had those from whom you wrested the power (rather, I would say,
whom you *deprived of* power : *wrested* implies conflict, and conflict there was none) understood and valued those rights.[1]   Anyhow, the bourgeois class which, amid much braying (principally on

---

[1] But, indeed, in our upper and middle classes there are many (perhaps they
form the majority) who are, to the eye that can see, but saxons " writ large "—
persons that differ in no respect from 'Arry (whose notion of " fun " is to have a
shy at a street lamp when the policeman is out of the way—which he very often
is)—save, indeed, that they have money in their pockets, and nothing in particular to do.—I declare this to be the most disgusting variety of the saxon
—yet he is a being whom you may meet even in the " upper circles " by
the score—brainless, ignorant, self-indulgent—his day's work some " sport " or
some game ;—give me, in preference, 'Arry of the third-class carriage on Bank
holiday, whose inarticulate yells—from drunkenness or mere good spirits—make
life for the time a torture to all who are near him.   Yes, the languid, lolling,
ignorant lout, the Gurth of the ball-room and the Row ; again, the moiling
and toiling ignorant Gurth of the counting-house (who will explain to you that he
takes no interest in politics) ; lastly, the ignorant Gurth of the country mansion,
who differs from Gurth his huntsman only by the accident of an accident—
these all must, in the nature of things, *pass away.*

the part of those who *conferred* the " boon ") received preponder-
ating power in 1832, seems to have by 1884 become—through
attaining physical comfort, money, leisure—so debilitated that it
did not even *know* the value of that which you last year removed from its nerveless hand.[1]   But although this is the case,
you were not justified in removing power from this bourgeois-
Gurth. You are not justified in robbing a miser. In other words,
you ought to have *gone to the constituencies*[2] before you introduced your franchise measure. In mere decency, and not to set
the precedent to aftertimes of a representative body snapping its
fingers at its creator and going on to " disestablish " that creator,
you ought to have taken the " opinion of the country."[3]   By
your act representative government, for all time, has received a
knock-down blow.

And now, when you have got your new Parliament, what can
you do with it ?   Do you find it an efficient legislative machine ?
Did you ever see, or read of, such a body of men professing to be
legislators ?   No ! I should think you didn't.   I can tell you that
Praise-God-Barebones' Parliament was an "assembly of kings" compared to it ; and to find its fellow, you must go back to that grand
legislative body, the Senate of Rome, which made Caligula's horse
a consul. Where is the intellectual power—to go no further—in that
horde of saxons, that would ever enable them to differ with you as
to *any* measure which you regarded—for *any* reason—as necessary ?
On the other hand, you would be bound to follow them absolutely
within the region of their " mental " activity.   Do what you please

---

[1] But even that cowardly, ignorant, bourgeois-saxon class (which, when things
seemed going smoothly, took some weeks, I should think, to subscribe £3,000
to the Mansion House Fund, and when the looting of Regent Street *waked*
it a bit—sent the score to " £70,000 up" literally off the reel)—this class
will—when it is pillaged and plundered by form of law, as it was lately by
the "working man," helping himself without form of law—open its stupid eyes
to what it lost in 1885.

[2] But why talk to *you* of what you ought to have done as a *Constitutional*
administrator ?

[3] The "opinion of the country" is, *I* hold, not worth much ! But that
ought not to be *your* view. I resent your act. You have no business to pose
as the Minister of the People, while you commit acts which Strafford would
have been ashamed of. But—you know your public !

in Ireland or the Soudan ; but take care how you meddle with the
" working man's " *beer.* In other regions of political activity,
they would never dare to oppose you [1]—and as to their *assist-*
ance, wouldn't you be infinitely better without it ? In short,
your grand Franchise Act made Parliamentary government a farce,
and introduced the government of *one*—that is, *for the present*,
yourself.

Thus you made the saxon supreme in Parliament in so far as
the government of England is concerned. But you did more.
Ordinary common sense would have demonstrated that this was no
time to raise the question of the franchise—with Ireland in a state
of factitious, government-produced, but (*to all law-abiding, loyal*
people) dangerous ferment. One would have thought it wise to
postpone the question for a century, rather than take it up at that
particular time. But you—whom one of your admirers lately
described, in pleonastic phrase, as "*quite the most intelligent man*
in England"—thought otherwise ; you *would* raise at this juncture
the question of the franchise ! Well, looking at the matter without
reference to actual results, *for the results are purely disastrous—*
I am rather glad to say that your quite the most greatest amount
of intelligence *failed.* You and I have read of a statesman who—

" Steered too nigh the sands to boast his wit."

That may have been your case ; at any rate, I humbly thank
Providence that, *so far as you are concerned*, your statesmanship is
hopelessly aground ; the seas are breaking over it, and the rotten
thing (with all its Plimsoll's marks) will presently go to pieces.—
It was bad enough to deprive *me* of the English franchise and
"thrust it upon" Gurth, my gatekeeper. Your act was uncon-

---

[1] Of course, they sometimes embarrass you, but always *under leadership ;* as
in the case of the vote for the " Royal " Parks above mentioned. When your
Franchise Bill was about to become law, one of your supporters met my
objection that the new electors would not understand anything about the
duties thrust upon them—by explaining that "*they would be well led*"—that is,
by the local caucus or wire-pullers. In other words, you put powers of
mischief into a man's hand, and yet he is not to be anything but a tool in the
hands of *a few !* See how near triumphant democracy is to tyranny !—I think
it well to record such "reasonings " here ; for we shall presently be face to
face with their like in this Irish business.

stitutional, tyrannical, high-handed, unjust.   But *you gave it to the Celt in Ireland,—that was* INSANE.   Gurth is no doubt our master ; but he is a stupid master ; he is like an ox ; he doesn't know his power.   And besides, the idea that he can't annihilate *us* and live himself might *ultimately* get into his thick head.   Anyhow, he is, in a sense, one of ourselves, and has got to rule or be ruled *here*.

But be this as it may, and with no wish to extenuate the folly of making our home-grown, artificially-manured barbarian the master of our destinies, I affirm that the act of extending the privilege of the franchise *to the Celt* transcended a hundred-fold, in wickedness and folly, the act of *dis*franchising *me* and *en*franchising my gatekeeper.   But French Revolutionism would have it so.   The man-and-brother Lie had to take another step in its mischievous career,—it had to be magnified and glorified ; and a being who— as towards my existence, the existence of my gatekeeper, and the existence of our entire community—might be more fitly termed a sleepless, unscrupulous *fiend—he* is intrusted with our national destiny ![1]   If we had no connection whatever with him, if he lived in some islands of the Pacific Archipelago, if we had no civil relation with him, all would be well.[2]—But he is at our doors— he is in the midst of us—*a foreign body*.   Well, in the hand of an enemy such, and so advantageously stationed to work our ruin, you placed a loaded pistol—which, *of course—naturally—necessarily* and as anybody but "quite the most intelligentest man in England " might have foreseen—he immediately pointed at the head of the idiot—(marked down for destruction !) who gave him the chance.

"When sin hath conceived, it bringeth forth *death*."   That man-and-brother lie and *perhaps* the desire to retain office (which, in a statesman, works all the evil effects of a lie, for to retain office is no *primary* wish of a true statesman) induced you, against

---

[1] The Celt is not, I repeat, in and by himself formidable,—but formidable only because of the ever-contemptible cowardice of the saxon-*sansculotte* government.

[2] Some people have benevolently wished that Ireland could be submerged for twenty-four hours.   But they don't know how much we should lose in losing the Celt.   As leaven in the lump of dull saxonism, he is invaluable.   The real evil is that the saxon can't manage the Celt ; and will in the future be ever less and less able to manage him.

the warnings and forebodings of the more sober and sensible
of your own followers, to invite (virtually) the bitterest enemy
England has ever had, has now, or can ever have—to enter the
citadel of the Empire and *there* to work his will.[1]

He has already worked his will ; and with what result? Why,
that you are now face to face with the Irish Difficulty in a FORM
TOTALLY INSOLUBLE—ON THIS SIDE REVOLUTION ! *You* going to
propose a series of measures for the "settlement" of the Irish
question ! No, sir ; nothing of the kind. You surely *cannot* be
so infatuated as to suppose that you (or any successor of yours in
"power") will now be anything but a tool of the Irish party in
the House of Commons—to be used for the destruction of the
Empire? I don't profess to understand the way your mind works :
considerations which to me and, I should think, to all mankind,[2]

[1] Some of the more fatuous or profligate among your followers (and perhaps
even you yourself) argued, in order to get your Franchise Bill passed, that it
would ruin Mr. Parnell's power in Ireland !! And they argued, too, that in the
"great" Land Bill of 1881 you would, by giving the tenant more than the
Land League could promise him, "dish" the Land League !!! Sir, there
are LIES which are very significant—significant, ominous, of *fate ;* and these
are of them. The lovers and makers of these lies—lies which denote such
idiocy and such villany—and the community that swallows them, are alike
bound for the pit of destruction.—It does not require the *event* to enable one
to ask : *Did your Land Act dish the Parnellites ?*—the Land Act which, these
LIARS must have known, or ought to have known, was the *creation of the
Parnellites.* And did the Franchise Act "dish" the Parnellites? How
effectually the Franchise Act dished (not the Parnellites but) the Gladstonian
"Liberals"—let poor T. Dickson tell.—While the Franchise Bill was looming
up, I had a talk with a well-known Liberal near Gweedore (the region that
owns the mild sway of the Rev. Father James McFadden, whom God preserve !).
I expressed my conviction that a Franchise Act, extended to Ireland, would
place the whole game in the hands of the Parnellites. "Ah, but," replied
my 'Liberal' Mentor, "don't you see"—and then he went on to affirm
that by a *Redistribution* measure, the Parnellites would be completely
"dished"—*positively* this time. In fact, he gave the impression that the
Franchise and Redistribution measures were two traps—fatal to the Parnellites,—set and baited by what we have since been instructed to call "an
old parliamentary hand" !—The "dishing" of the Parnellites is like the rain-
bow—always in the next field.

[2] Except to some of your own following, who apparently "follow" your logic
—or perhaps only "swallow" your "conclusions"? Some of these people explained to me, when the Franchise Bill was going through the Houses, that nobody could say whether it would give Mr. Parnell a majority—"*No, not so sure*

seem obvious—so obvious that we should not think of mentioning them—things, in short, that go without saying,—these considerations, opinions, anticipations, forebodings, are met by your henchmen with a smile—and they go on to deny what is as clear as the conclusion of a syllogism in *Barbara.*—How you can *now* conceit yourself a free agent is more than I can make out. I suppose, too, you would deny that you are the author—the sole author—of this state of things ! Very well.—Now let us make a few deductions based on this Franchise Act of yours ; your denial will go in each case along with our affirmation, and the *event* will decide which of us is right.

1. You bring in a measure *which will not please the Irishry.*

Conclusion : You will be roaming—officeless—among the few trees still "spared" at Hawarden in one month,—your premiership "ancient history," and your influence as dead as Chelsea.[1] You deny that ?—Good.

2. Every future Government—of whatever class or party—will hold office under precisely the same conditions—that is, it will, if it would retain power securely for *one week*, have to be ready to do its level best to get the Irishry the moon if they cry for it—even though they should raise the cry in pure "devilment."

You deny the validity of this deduction ?—Very good.

3. You bring in a measure which *will* please the Irishry.

Conclusion : You smash the Empire.

You deny that conclusion also ?—Excellent-good.

---

about that"!!—But even if it *did*, the two English parties in the House would, don't you know, *if either gained a majority by the Parnellite vote*, agree to act *precisely as if that vote had not been given.* Well, though this is a strange view of government by majorities, we know that the compact has been carried out ! *Of course*, Lord Salisbury is still Prime Minister, and you are sitting on the Opposition side of the House. *Of course* you refused office, because you *would have been placed in office by the Parnellite vote*,—not to mention your determination never to owe power to such a criminal lunacy as Mr. Jesse Collings's Amendment. And *of course*, when Lord Salisbury now says something about his party being out of office, significant looks are exchanged between the members of his family, and a paragraph will, I suppose, get into the newspapers to the effect that Lord S.'s health is such as to cause considerable anxiety to his friends !

[1] For the very good reason that the only influence you now *can* wield depends upon the favour or toleration of the Irish party.

These, then, are my affirmations, with your denials tacked on. I willingly abide the decision of *events*, because, in arguing as to your former activity—in pointing out the rottenness of the initial principle, and then the inevitably disastrous result, I was open to the retort (a very silly one, but if there were not many thousands of silly—*and therefore mischievous*—people in these islands, we should not be in our present plight)—that it was "the wisdom that comes after the event." It was *not* that sort of wisdom ; but no matter. Here we are face to face with a new bit of your activity, and our relation to it is this : we know the *cause*—your Franchise Act,—but we don't know the *effect*—in the sense that it is not palpably before our eyes as a *fait accompli*. Now, summing up, I affirm generally, that—

1. Your Franchise Act, by extending the right of voting to the class *in England* which you "enfranchised," has ruined the British Parliament as a body qualified to administer efficiently the affairs of the British Empire.

2. Your Franchise Act, by extending the right of voting to the class in Ireland which you enfranchised, has made Parliamentary Government in England impossible, and has presented you with only *two possible* issues :—Revolution or Dismemberment.

3. Your Franchise Act, by extending the right of voting to these two classes in Ireland and England, will be as fatal in its effects, though you, the author of it, should cease this very hour to discharge the functions of a responsible statesman.

Since, then, your Franchise Act is such and so mischievous, I look forward to your *proposals* to be presently made with absolute indifference. You vaulted into office on the Parnellite vote, you are maintained there by the same agency,—and all your successors will hold office on the same terms—" *durante bene placito*" and " *quamdiu se bene gesserint* "—the autocratic body to be pleased, and who will graciously, if it should be so minded, pronounce the approving word " *bene* " in regard to the actions of English statesmen being—the Irish party. In short, you "carry on the Queen's government" *in obedience to every whim of the Queen's enemies.* Under these circumstances, why talk of " measures "—" proposals "—as if you were any longer a free agent? *You are bound to surrender.* Thus the Empire at once touches the point which you, on a memorable occasion, indicated by the words " disintegration and dismemberment." *Les voici !* [1]

So much, then, as to your activities in the past, and their results ; —so much as to your late activity and *its* results—which are yet to come. I humbly think that the ground I took up at the outset I have maintained ; and that my assertion, *that your present attempt to settle the Irish Difficulty will result in disastrous failure,* has been proved to a demonstration.

I have now, sir, said my say on your *record* in regard to the Irish question ; and *I find it impossible to believe that you will propose any measures bearing ever so remotely* " EVEN IN THE DIRECTION " *of a solution of it.*[2] I will next try to formulate the phenomena of mind and character revealed in the several acts that make up your record, in order to ascertain whether your failures have been necessary or only accidental. Our conclusions under this head will either confirm, or lead us to modify, the conclusions derived from your record looked at by itself, and without reference to the mind and character of the agent. By way of illustration : Take that grand figure—one of the grandest in all history—the great Semitic strategist and tactician—Hannibal. He was a man of war from his youth. But he had not such a run of good fortune as, say, our Marlborough or Wellington.

Look now, lastly, at the qualities of mind and character in you, this record of yours reveals :—they show that the solution of the Difficulty by YOU is impossible— unthinkable.

---

[1] Now mark—when the inevitable crash comes, it won't do for your followers to look very innocent, or, if they speak, to point out that such a result could not have been anticipated by any human foresight, or argued to by any.human power of reasoning. *Littera scripta manet :* this plain tale will *be there* to put them down !

[2] And in statesmanship few actions are *indifferent*—neither good nor bad. Usually, actions *in themselves* indifferent, or only at worst silly, become in statesmanship grave wrongs. That " Suakim-Berber Railway " project was *in itself* a bit of mere objectless foolery,—decided upon, for anything we know, as the Crimean expedition was " decided upon "—when the majority of the Cabinet were dozing after dinner—at which dinner some had, doubtless, dined " not wisely but too well." Anyhow, the expedition to the Crimea cost about £80,000,000, I have been told. And this single item of the " Suakim-Berber Railway " cost somewhere about £1,000,000. That is, the British taxpayer will be burdened *for ever* with a yearly impost of £30,000, and all for a silly *fiasco.* But it's grand to feel that in England *the People* rule !—that we have no Prince Bismarck over us,—though when *he* expends a million sterling for a certain article, he first of all considers whether the article is worth the money, and having decided that it is—*he sees that he gets it.*

He was the victor at Cannæ; he was defeated at Zama. Alas, he ended his military career *in defeat*. Very well; then he showed some weakness at Zama?[1] Not a bit of it. He showed as superb generalship at Zama as he had shown at Cannæ and Trasimenus. In defeat and in victory he was *the world's greatest general*. Now, how can I make this assertion? On what grounds do I base it? On an examination *of his record*.[2] I find running through it all, in defeat as in victory, the manifestations of *a certain set of powers*—and this phenomenon is ever present. So that I could almost *predict* what Hannibal would be likely to do. At any rate, I could tell what he would *not* do : he would not do anything *stupid*. I could predict that if there was the slightest weakness in the generalship of his opponent, the Carthaginian would have his finger on the weak spot in an instant! On the other hand, if his unfortunate (*necessarily* unfortunate) opponent should try "forward play" with Hannibal, I could be *absolutely certain* that he would be very soon knocked out of time. His forward play would probably

---

[1] This is the amount of perception that the saxon shows in dealing with those who serve him. *Nothing succeeds like success.* Govern Scotland Yard for seventeen years in such a manner that no man can raise a finger against you. Then, let a totally irrelevant *accident* occur, a block, say, on the Highland Railway,—an accident, however, which the saxon "mind" *somehow* connects—be it ever so remotely—with *you*, and official saxondom will dance in terror for its own skin till it fingers your resignation. How much more noble the early Roman, who received home with acclamations a *beaten general :* and *why ?* Because, in all his defeats, he had shown that he had never once "despaired of the republic"! I make no doubt there were "Romans" so "saxon" in their feelings that they would have measured worth —military ability—solely *by success*. But they were not official persons, nor regarded as very "capable citizens."

[2] It is a strange fact that the glorious generalship of this ἄναξ ἀνδρῶν—if ever such existed—that his great exploits—should be reported solely by *his enemies*. His own community—which was as unworthy of him as the Saxon community in the ninth century was unworthy of glorious Alfred—left no record of him or anybody else. It passed away and made no sign. What would become of the reputation of an English general who had over and over again defeated the French—if the French were the sole chroniclers of his deeds ?—But it is unfair to the truthful Romans to mention them in connection with such abandoned liars as the modern French—and especially the official French. Think of the tale of the *Vengeur,* of Cambronne's *mot* at Waterloo, of the *French* account of the battle of the Alma, &c.

develope his overthrow, even though Hannibal had been, before this folly, hard put to it to see how he was to act.[1]—Then, again, in regard to *Nicias*, you could be as certain from *his* previous record—his record *before* he sailed on that fatal Sicilian Expedition—that nothing but disaster could come of it. You would, from the study of his previous record, have arrived at conclusions as to his mind and character which would have compelled you—with the best will in the world towards him as an individual—to believe that the Expedition was *doomed.*

What quality of mind and character appears, as a sort of common factor, at every step in your record? I answer : *a total absence of principle.* Don't misunderstand me. I have told you before that I don't care a *traneen* what your morals, principles, or acts are—in private life. If I had been an Athenian at the epoch of the Sicilian Expedition, I should have preferred Alcibiades to Nicias if I had thought he would capture Syracuse. I have said already that the business of a steersman is—not to show piety, nor philanthropy, nor to lecture me on Temperance, nor to solve the problem of the Universe, nor to ascertain where all the pins go,—but—*to steer.* If he steers well, that is all I want ; if he doesn't steer well, it makes no matter what else he does well ; and if I see a steady, consistent vice in his steering—I must tell him so. And if the vessel, under his guidance, behaves as the new *Agamemnon* did on her first run down Channel—in which she was prevented from ramming the Admiralty pier at Dover, only by risking a smash against Cape Gris-Nez,—I am bound to do all I can to remove that steersman. and take chance of putting a better in his place.—Your weakness, as I have said, is—*want of principle.* That is the quality *which runs through your whole record.* What I mean is—that there does not seem to be any line of policy which—I do not say on proper reason shown, but on *sufficient pressure brought*—you are not prepared to adopt or to abandon ! Well, sir, if this observation of your character represent the

[1] Compare Cromwell's exclamation as he saw Leslie's troops (though against Leslie's will) try "forward play" at Dunbar :—"The Lord hath delivered them into my hand !"—Oh, sir, that we had, as a people, such a record in statesmanship as we have, if not in generalship, at least in soldiership and seamanship !

actual fact (and there is not a man in England who *desires* to find it less a fact than I do)—your statesmanship *must* be one consistent *failure*.   A heathen poet who lived two thousand years ago—before the French Revolution and before the promulgation of Christianity—marked out the "*Justum ac* TENACEM PROPOSITI *virum*" as the man, and the only man, fitted to do great things. You are the antithet of that character ; your public actions on this question, and in many other regions of political activity, have been consistently *unjust*,[1] and your *tenacity* is exactly measured by the amount of pressure you have received from without.   Being such, your activity must, I repeat, prove one consistent *failure*.   From the era of that Clerkenwell explosion which led you to ruin the Irish Church—through the time when you waved the telegram in the air at the Lord Mayor's banquet, and announced that "the resources of civilisation" were sufficient to cope with the evils in Ireland—when he who was, by the testimony of your own Attorney-General, "steeped to the lips in treason," walked out of prison a free man, his powers of mischief enormously increased—when, again, you asked—"*what was meant by Home Rule?—you were willing to entertain the question*"—down to the day when you entered office, to *hold* office on condition that *you* should tell what Home Rule means, and that Mr. Parnell should "entertain" your view or not, as he liked,—through all this period—in your every act, you are seen, not looking to any *principle* of public policy—but yielding, now here, now there, to shifting phenomena of external pressure.[2]

---

[1] Not, observe, that *you* are *consistently* anything.   But *it happens* that the pressure applied to you in our degenerate times has been "consistent" in always driving you towards *injustice*.   You have simply yielded to the *force majeure*. Circumstances drove you to measures which originated and developed the party of American-Irish Jacobinism ; circumstances forced you to make that party supreme in the State ; and circumstances now compel you to "govern" the State at their bidding.

[2] One of the most extraordinary defences ever set up was that by which your followers explained and excused your bloody and absolutely pointless and irrelevant "policy" in the Soudan, by saying that *you had yielded* to the clamour of the Tory party !!   The Tory party are naturally bloodthirsty—and they forced you to engage in "military operations" !   But how is it that the "greatest statesman of the age" carries out the policy of his "wicked" opponents ?

And if you have, at the present moment, yielded *all* to Rebellion,
—you have done so because Rebellion has known how to keep
a steady pressure upon you—while the wretched saxons, squab-
bling among themselves, and thinking (!)—thinking "there must
be something in" this cry for Home Rule, are really the *allies*
of those who, in carrying out a sham, can smash an empire.—
As at home so abroad. Komaroff and Joubert, Austria after your
"hands off" indiscretion—these played the same steady, forward
game which Mr. Parnell is such a master of,—and they won and
were bound to win.

Now, I need not say that "total absence of principle" would
never *announce* itself in plain terms *as such*. If it did,
even the being I have called *the saxon* would be able to see
that something was wrong! No: your failure to seize, and
stick to a principle, appears in forms very well calculated to
deceive your Caliban following. *You are inconsistent,*—but to
conclude that a man is inconsistent, one must *ascertain, recollect,
compare* the successive phenomena of his record—a series of
activities out and beyond any powers possessed by our poor
saxon to compass. Therefore, you can be—as towards your
followers—safely inconsistent,—but not *to us*.

Again, being totally destitute of political principle, you must,
having nothing to which you can *cling,*—cling through good and evil
report, through thick and thin—cling hard and fast, cling as the
limpet to the rock—cling, no matter what befalls,—you must, I say,
be driven from pillar to post, in sheer, desperate desire to find out
something that will make for your safety! But this will seem, whatever *you* may call it, to outsiders mere *timidity*. And, looking
to your record, nothing is so striking a feature in it as this same
timidity. It really seems as if any *hare* in the kingdom possessed
more pluck, more force, than you!

Coupled with this hare-like timidity in the presence of *pressure
consistently applied,*—which timidity arises, I insist, from incapacity to seize a *principle*, and hold it against all opposition, hold it, cling to it, were it but with the finger-nails—
from the mature conviction that it is *sound*, and *must*, therefore, bring a man peace at the last—coupled, I say, with this
essential and fatal weakness of character is the most absolute

apparent [1] belief in yourself, and in the efficacy of your successive
"measures." You *seem* to think that what you propose will, in each
case, prove a remedy! Such a power of self-deception is without
parallel. But more ; your "remedy" having *necessarily* failed, failed
before all men and before the sun—what becomes of you? Do
you retire into private life? Do you retire even from *official* life?
No! you are again to the fore with another—this positively the
last—"remedy." And when this, too, *necessarily* fails—you are
again ready—and so on, to *n* times! [2]—Now, such astounding
self-confidence in proposing "measures" is really equivalent to
sheer *insanity* when the measures have reference to the Irish
question.—But this quality of self-confidence is dangerous not only
to yourself, but to the saxon herd that looks up to you for
guidance. The saxon, utterly indisposed to master—or incapable of mastering—the elements of the Irish problem (I
have called him a papist and you his political pope), is constrained to fall back on you ; and thus, for so far, we have
—as the constituent elements of all the "solvent" England
can produce :—Rudderless want of principle, hare-like timidity,
measureless audacity, these in the leading agent,—and in the
body that is to give effect to the proposals that are the re-
sultant of all these forces—stupid, swine-like ignorance ! Really,
now, if the Irish Problem submitted to solution in the presence
of such "solvents "—all I can say is, *it ought to be ashamed of itself.*

Another quality, clearly discernible in all your activity, is a power

---

[1] I say *apparent*, because I cannot *see* how it can be *real*. I cannot take in the
idea. But human character is full of such (apparent) contradictions, that
a man who now flings another into gaol for a certain "offence," and
now humbly accepts office from the same man and constitutes himself the agent
in carrying out the policy for proclaiming which, in much milder terms, that
man was said to be "steeped to the lips in treason" and thrown into prison
with flaunts of telegram and saxon cheering—may possibly *to himself* be
steady, consistent—nay, the just and tenacious man of Horace's encomium !

[2] I hope you don't suppose that in this, or in any other of your acts, I *blame*
you. Blame is out of the question. If, *after repeated failures*, the "country"
calls you to *fail again*,—that is the country's affair. And if you are willing to
come forward and *fail again*, that is your affair. And the mistake of the
"country" and your own mistake will be duly visited by a Power that forgives
a *failure* as little as it forgives a *sin*. Where is blame then ?—*It is excluded.*

of calling *any* thing by *any name* that suits the exigency of the
moment. I have noticed this characteristic before ; but I am now
formally examining your whole mind *as evidenced in your actions*,
with the view of arriving at a conclusion as to the likelihood of
your proposing anything to the purpose at the present juncture. I
suppose this quality is connected with that other, which is also very
manifest in your record—of attaining, in public speech, with due,
though very involved, syntax, an absolute *unintelligibility* in
respect of matter. Macaulay noticed this quality in his Review
of your book on "Church and State." You seem to be the
victim of your own sentence-making, and are an example of
Bacon's assertion that, whereas we believe we are masters of the
language we employ, the language we employ, in reality, often
masters us. But that vague, cloudy, hazy, fogging, bewildering,
chloroforming style—be its origin what it may [1]—is not the style
that would characterize the man who could tackle the Irish Difficulty with any hope of success.—Incapacity to call a spade a spade
may arise from one of three sources—a mental, a moral, or a linguistic source,—and the man who labours under this incapacity from
any source must be, so far forth, *weak*—perhaps ridiculous, perhaps
mischievous. He may not *know* that a certain thing is called a
spade, though he may know the *word* "spade." Then that word
is a bit of mere lumber in his mind ; and it may become mischievous : he may, on occasion, apply it to a spade, a banjo, or a
chest of drawers. Or he may know that the thing *ought* to be
called a spade,—but *it may not suit him* to call it a spade. This
is worse. Or he may not know the word *spade*. In any view of
the matter he is distinctly *weak*. And a weak man, even in the
matter of using words, is not the man to settle the Irish question.
If his incapacity arises from mental feebleness, he is in bad case ;

[1] Many people hold that this peculiarity in your utterances arises from a
deliberate intention to mystify, delude,—just as they hold that the central
quality of your character is egoism, and your *one consistent and persistent
wish*—in your capacity of statesman—to obtain and retain power ! If their
theories be correct, there is no mystery about the matter. But I don't accept
their theories ; I prefer to let the phenomenon be, for me, *inexplicable*. As
for this nebulous sentence-making—Macaulay noticed it at a period in your
career when you can scarcely be supposed to have deliberately determined to
fog the public.

if from moral obliquity, he is done for. He must *here* speak plainly, as well as act squarely.

Another, possibly dangerous, characteristic is—your piety, conscientiousness, " good intentions," and—" all that sort of thing." Don't misunderstand me. Piety and conscientiousness are, on the whole, very good things in themselves; but, as I have before intimated, they may become dangerous qualities in a statesman. Does anybody doubt the piety, conscientiousness and good intentions of the heads of the Inquisition ?—The truth is, there is no more helpless victim of self-deception than the pious man—who sees in all his notions, whims, caprices, the leading of Providence, and who can, relying on the arrogant assumption that Providence (as well as *justice*) "has been his guide," behold with unmoved countenance the ravages, for example, that your measures—the direct outcome of piety and good intention—have wrought in ever-miserable Ireland.—Then, there is the danger that arises from the *effect* that conspicuous piety produces on silly minds. A pious man is, *to me*, a man who is likely to go to heaven; but his mere *piety* gives me no assurance that he will conduct with success any business I may entrust to him in this vale of tears. I might have many occasions to wish him fairly with Christ, which, for me as well as for him, would perhaps be "far better." Statesmanship and "other-worldliness" are not incompatible, but statesmanship is essentially a thing of *this* world. On the other hand, silly people—the people (unfortunately) forming the bulk of "the population of these islands "—if we may trust Carlyle— are mightily taken with piety, or even the semblance of piety. If a man is *pious* (so they "argue"), he must be *right*. Strange to say, I argue that if he is *aggressively* pious, he is very likely *to be wrong. Remember Nicias.* Remember what the Athenians suffered through trusting to *his* piety.—Piety, then, is a quality which is, at best, irrelevant, and *may be* dangerous, in a statesman.

Well, summing up under this head, in which I have been ascertaining the mental and moral qualities revealed in the several acts of your record I find—That now, when *for the third time* you stand up to this Irish problem, your mental and moral *apparatus* for solving it are :—a total *absence of principle*, showing itself in *hare-like timidity*, and *utter inconsistency*, which yet puts on the guise of *absolute certainty* and *self-confidence;* these qualities—united with a power of glamouring and fogging, perhaps yourself, certainly your followers, through *a peculiar use of language*—united, also, with manifested *piety* and *conscientiousness* and oft-proclaimed *good intentions.*

Sir, that a man with these qualities—these " gifts and graces " should now " settle " that Irish question which, by the very exercise of these qualities, gifts, and graces, he has made insoluble *on this side Revolution*—is *absolutely unthinkable.*

IV.

THE RIGHT MAN—AND THE SOLUTION.

IT is now high time to bring these remarks to a close. The last I proceed to indicate, then, in conclusion :— object of our inquiry is—What sort of man is needed at the present crisis ; and *what would he do in order to solve the difficulty?*

1. The man who would solve the difficulty, in so far as it could (i.) the sort of man required for the solution of the Difficulty ; be solved by an individual, must be a man of clear mental insight, inflexible resolution, patience, persistence, courage and unswerving honesty.   Now, that looks, I admit, very like one of the platitudes that we are so familiar with in journals that support your various policies.   But let us go on: let us see what this man's *mental insight* will enable him to perceive, and his *unswerving honesty* [1] enable him to carry out.—and whether his policy is like yours.

[1] Let me say, in passing, that we have in those two qualities—the qualities of a man who, and who alone, could solve the Irish problem. The only other element requisite is—Time.—But in our wretched yet self-conceited community —where is the *mental insight?*—where the *unswerving honesty?* And even if we were fortunate enough to secure these qualities, *how long* would the statesman possessing them be permitted to retain power? Lord Salisbury in a few months *saved England from war* (I know what I am talking about), yet Lord Salisbury goes out (ostensibly, at least) because he won't sul mit to Mr. Jesse Collings's criminal-lunatic amendment !   You see our method of Government lacks *continuity.*   Very well : we pay for that with an Irish Question *now* absolutely insoluble.

He has studied (we must assume) all that in literature bears upon government ; and he has studied, at first hand, human Nature and human History, with the view of finding whether the Reign of Law extends to the phenomena of Human Society,—and if so, what are the Laws, economic, social, political, that are unmistakably manifest. Having done so, he goes on to ascertain and throw into formula the origin and function *of the State.* He ascertains (I am certain) that *the sole function of the State,*— that for which the State was called into being, is—TO PROTECT PROPERTY— this and nothing else. He will look at this result of his studies and arguings on all sides. Instead of the function—*to protect property*, he will substitute *other* functions, and carefully *work out* the sum till he arrives at the answer. He will substitute *e.g.*—*to make all—or any—members of the community comfortable.* This he will reject at once : it can't be done without resorting to *plunder.* (See above.) So of such substitutions as—*to educate the people, to provide amusement for the people, to make the people sober, moral, religious,*[1] &c. &c.—and in every such case he will, working out the problem, arrive at an impossibility or an absurdity. Then, coming back and examining again the conclusion which asserts that the function of the State is *to protect property,*—trying it by any the most stringent tests that he has employed on the other conclusions, he finds that this conclusion—and this alone —*bears all such tests.*[2]

Having settled all this after due (and it probably would be long) study and cogitation, he feels that he has taken a step in the direction of " settling" questions of government. *He has arrived at a " fundamental law."* He need not open *that* book again. He is not so " excessively *candid* " as to entertain any questioning in

[1] Poor W. E. Forster, in one of his latest speeches, committed himself to the *amusement* fallacy !

[2] And this would be the " note " of his activity to the end. He would grasp *principles* and *apply* principles. He would *prescribe* the particular pattern of every tap in the engine, but he wouldn't lose time *turning* every tap ; his assistants could do that—but, come what might, he would see that the engine had that in it which would make it *go.*—What colleague of yours could have taken charge of any of your " great" measures? If anything had happened to you during the passage of, *e.g.*, your Land Bill of 1881,—what would have become of that pernicious folly ? It would have tumbled to pieces on the floor of the House ! Very well : *that shows the measure was rotten.*

regard to a problem he has so carefully worked out, and the truth of which he sees demonstrated by *events* every day he rises. To open his " book " again would seem to him childish loss of time.

He then takes a step ahead, and concludes further—that if the sole function of the State is *to protect property*, the sole function of the Statesman is to fight against,—to burn, sink, and destroy those degenerate elements in the community [1] that would deprive men of *their property*—the thing for which they make all the exertions of their life,—the thing which not even the robbers of the community, in high or low station, will give up if they can help it.[2]

The conclusion that the State exists for the protection of property involves this other : that the State is *subsequent* to the individual, and exists for the benefit of the individual—that is, for the benefit of the individual whose property is to be protected, and who contributes his quota of property towards the support of the State [3]—not for the benefit of those who choose to land in the State from another country, or from any quarter whatever. And this Statesman would observe that the wealth and happiness of the community increase in proportion as the individual is free to use his special activity.

This being the case, he would not trouble himself much about *forms* of government. He would not accept the poet's silly formula :—" Each best administered is best." Rather he would say—Each government which enables every honest citizen to live in the greatest safety alike from foreign and domestic foes — *that* is the best. But whatever form of polity *arose naturally* from the circumstances and necessities of the case—whatever

---

[1] These must exist in larger or smaller amount in all communities, but the action of the community can increase them so as to enable them to bring the community to ruin.

[2] The damnable hypocrisy of the apostles of plunder is manifest when the garotter from Whitechapel or St. Stephen's " puts on the hug "—on *them*.

[3] A *wise* government would exert its energies—not in devising schemes to rob the worthy, and to protect (and thereby *increase*) the unworthy, but in devising and carrying out a "scheme" by which every man living in the community, and reaping the benefits of civilized life, would, according to his power, be made *to pay* for his advantages !—The highest effort of modern "statesmanship" results in making A. pay for B. !—But what will become of B. when A. emigrates—or ceases *to be able* to pay for B. ? (See above.)

form had most of nature, and least of artificiality about it, *that*
he would approve.[1]   Because, in such a state of things, his
primary object, *the protection of the property of the individuals
who contribute to the burdens of the State* would approach nearer
to *absolute attainment.*   Any developments in the form of government of his own country he would accept when they arose slowly,
that is, naturally—provided the primary object of government
were all the better secured by such changes.   But all changes, all
"measures," tending to make the primary object more difficult
of attainment he would abhor, and as far as possible fight against
—to the point of taking up arms and proving that force *is* a
remedy.

Again, he would hold that it is a good thing in a State to have
as little Government as possible—regarding it as in itself an
evil, though a necessary evil—necessary because and only because
of the existence of certain degenerate organisms in the community.[2]

Lastly, there being in his blood no sewer gas of French Revolutionism, he would not be, and could not be, the victim of such
pernicious Lies as I have already catalogued.   (See page 15.)

Called to administer the affairs of the Empire, he considers,
first and foremost, that his duty is *to the Empire, as he finds it.*
It would be no business of his to inquire, for instance, how we
came by India or Gibraltar or Malta or Cyprus or Ireland.   The
sole consideration which weighs with him is—*we possess them.*
He considers the exclamation, "perish India," as a most traitorous
utterance in the mouth of a responsible British statesman.   When
our material resources and our fighting power *failed* to hold

---

[1] For example, he would not commit the absurdity of supposing that our
English constitution has in it something *sa red*, and that wherever it is introduced it must make everybody happy!   He would (*on absolutely rational
grounds*) sympathise with Prince Bismarck and Count Von Moltke in their
endeavours to make Germany *formidable*.   For he would understand (as those
really great men do) that Germany, with France on the one side and Russia on
the other, must be either *formidable* or extinct, either a *terror* or a non-
entity!   For my part, may Germany long be a *terror* in Europe—a terror
to all scoundrel-statesmen—at home or abroad!

[2] Needless to say he would do nothing *to multiply* such organisms—the sole
"function" which our Government seems capable of discharging—and *at the
cost* of *really* "capable citizens"!

India—then he would reluctantly give it up.   But he would give it up because he *couldn't hold it.*   No treason *there.*

Summoned to look after the affairs of Ireland, he would (knowing the entire history of Ireland —all the big lies [1] and all the small bits of truth in it, knowing the people, moreover, *by actual contact with them*) [2]—he would, I say, carry with him his simple principle—*protect property.*   Any "*ascendency*"?   None.   He knows no ascendency save the "ascendency" of the *true man* over the idler, the thief.   And he knows that if he (which is inconceivable) sides with the thief—he, but much more the community—would *pay for it.*   He does not, by way of putting an end to *this* ascendency, by way of "*steering an even keel*," adopt the saxon method of shifting to the *other* side cargo, shot and shell, coals, guns, ballast, crew—everything, in short, that could bring the gunwale under.—He doesn't commit the absurdity of prosecuting members of Parliament and others for "treasonable" speeches.   He lets every man in Ireland say what he likes.   What, he would ask, has *talk* to do with *the protection of property?*   "*Well, but* (this is the wisdom of *your* school of politicians—if you belong to any school) *they incite*—those men who make inflammatory speeches and write inflammatory articles, such as those in *United Ireland* —*they incite* to outrage."   To which our statesman—being a very direct person—able and *inclined* to call a spade a spade and only that—would probably reply, in Mr. Burchell's formula —*Fudge.*—Let me catch any one subject of Her Majesty injuring any other subject of Her Majesty in life, limb or store—and I won't ask who *incited* him to the crime.   But till there is an *overt act*, I have no business to interfere. 'Can't you let things alone?'   If you don't ask the criminal,

---

[1] From the lie that it was ever, *in ancient times,* called "Insula Sacra" save by a linguistic blunder, down to the latest—which I don't pretend to know ; or that it had any settled government from the day one of its chiefs fled to Julius Agricola to the day when Dermot MacMorragh invited Henry the Second to undertake the conquest of it—always excepting what the "Danes" had done in the direction of civilization.   If the Danes had been more numerous, there would be now no Irish question.

[2] Not requiring, like you, to be in office in order to be aware of the state of Ireland !

who—what orator—what newspaper—"incited" him, and then
punish, not the actual criminal, but the orator whom he charges
with having incited him,[1]—*how can you*, in Heaven's name, prosecute a public speaker, or a journal, for uttering words that are
calculated to lead to outrage, &c. ? Let a man utter in public as
many "treasonable" speeches as he pleases ; let him incite to any
crime he pleases.[2]—" *Would you put down the National League ?* "
Well, had I (and not *you*) been in power at the time, the National
League would never have come into existence, no, nor the Land
League either.   Therefore, I am not *bound* to answer your
question ; but I *will* answer it, and my answer is—*Certainly not*.[3]
You don't seem to apprehend the nature and scope of Government.   Listen :—Government cannot institute an inquisition into
the minds and consciences, nor even all the *acts*, of men—it can
deal only with such offences as are borne witness to in open day ;
and its activity is limited to offences connected with *property*[4]
(which includes life).   It is a very rough and coarse instrument ;

---

[1] In which case you would have the interesting spectacle of a convicted
criminal turned into an untainted witness *against* (in all probability) a perfectly
innocent speaker or journal. Alas for grandmotherly government ! You go
but two steps back in order to demonstrate its rottenness !

[2] That is, provided the persons incited be of full age—not infants in the eye
of the law, or lunatics.—" *But*," you answer—"*that's the very thing! These
poor Irish peasants are very, very excitable ; and when these men and these
journals rouse their feelings, they, &c., &c. You see they are like children.*"
And yet, you have just given those "children"—300,000 of them—the
franchise ! Again, you prosecute Hyndman, Champion and the rest, for *talk*
in Trafalgar Square, instead of giving capable citizens "a whiff of grape-shot"
in Regent Street !

[3] Of course, this is, unfortunately, an imaginary sketch ; our statesman
assumes a *worthy England* behind him. By the way, it does not follow,
as matters stand, that Lord Salisbury's Government was wrong in its policy
in regard to the National League.

[4] " *Still harping on my daughter !* "—No, sir ! Harping on no daughter or
sister, cousin or aunt of yours ! Harping on *the sacredness of property*, which
is the key-stone—the indispensable condition—of civilization, and the cause
and chief end of all government !—When Land-Commissioners invade you (or
your descendants) at Hawarden, reduce or abolish your rents ; first build a
set of labourers' cottages within biscuit-throw of your drawing-room window,
and then forcibly expropriate you,—probably *then* you, or your representative
descendant, will come to understand why I go on harping on Property,
Property, Property.

it often fails—even in its own field of activity; but you don't improve it by applying it to what it was never intended to do.[1] You *cannot vitally affect* the National League—*as* a League. You *cannot*, in fact, suppress it. "*I am glad we agree in that, at any rate ; for we will not suppress the National League.*"—But we don't agree. *You* decline to suppress the National League because you are afraid of it ; and because you fear your suppression of it would end in your being turned out of office, which most certainly would be the case. You are afraid of it, and don't suppress it. *I* see nothing in it to be afraid of, and therefore I don't suppress it.— And besides, you are not consistent : you suppressed—amid much braying—the Land League—why not the National League, which is, of the two, *for you*, by far the more formidable ?[2]

"*But do you not concern yourself with Religion—with Education, &c. ?*" No. As for the first, Irishmen may go to—heaven their own way. Personally, I hope they will all go to heaven ; *I* wish I could see certain of them preparing with less assiduity to go to "another place." But as statesman, I have nothing to do with the matter,—nor have I anything to do with Education. Let anybody who wants education pay for it. The fact is—government with me is—not a pseudo-philosophical-humanitarian-rights-of-man, moral-religious-educational organization, which levies taxes from a brute-community, that does not know its right hand from its left, to support all my fads—but an *Insurance Society* against thieves, of which Insurance Society I am manager. I avoid two mistakes which you, and all your like, commit— (hence the Ireland which you see, and which, mark me, *you have made*). (1) Being manager of a Company insuring against thieves, I exact the lowest possible amount from those who insure, and I can afford to ask a very low figure, because I take on no *factitious duties ;* I decline to feed, clothe, and educate my clients, besides insuring them against thieves—and still more, to feed, clothe, and educate those who *don't* insure. Your mistake—and you will find it out very soon—

[1] Your Hawarden hatchet does well enough when you confine yourself to cutting down trees, but you don't shave with it.

[2] The reason is manifest : you had not, when you suppressed the Land League, put your neck, and England's neck, under the heel of the "Nationalist" party.

is—that you employ the premium paid by those who *bonâ fide* insure—to feed, clothe, and educate those who don't insure, and cannot insure. Besides, you have just now given this latter class a vastly preponderant voice on the Board of Directors! Can any good come of such an arrangement?—(2) But you have done more. You have given the casting vote in the management to the most formidable body of thieves in the United Kingdom,— and yet, people say you are now going (by the aid of those whom you feed, clothe, and educate, and also by the help of this syndicate of thieves) to "settle" all "Difficulties" of the Company![1]

(2) his policy of solution,

2. Thus far our statesman. Coming now to the SOLUTION of the Irish Problem, to which you have given so many days and nights—I observe that we are promised THREE measures (another Trinity-in-Unity) which, we are assured, will "settle" once for all this ever-recurrent Irish trouble. Alas for human hopes! The chances are ten thousand to one *against* your proposing *any* measure "bearing, ever so remotely, even in the direction" of a solution of the Irish Problem. I have examined your record; I have examined the leading qualities of your mind; I have examined, moreover, the *instrument* (forged by yourself) which you are compelled to use in this work—this "reformed" Parliament— and here, in my last pages, I am constrained to affirm that *you must fail.*

But as I desire to be, in my remarks, perfectly definite, clear, unmistakable (therefore, if wrong, easily refutable); as I wish that you may, if you are so minded, follow my suggestions now, and that I may recall them, if necessary, to your remembrance hereafter,— I will take the programme which you have announced, and say what you ought to propose under each of the three heads: SOCIAL ORDER, LOCAL "SELF"-GOVERNMENT, and THE LAND QUESTION.

But, first, I must observe that the very idea of your "settling" the Irish Question by any "measures" whatever, is the height of absurdity! You have an unaccountable belief in *machine-made* statesmanship. It does not seem ever to have occurred to you that there are certain things which are as far removed from the

---

[1] The most formidable "Difficulty" arising from the devilish activity of these same thieves—even *before* you made them autocratic!

region of "constructive statesmanship" as are the movements of Jupiter's satellites. Has the thought never crossed your mind that we mortals possess a dreadful power of *destruction*, but that our power of *reconstruction*—of *restitution*—is sadly limited, impressing on us the truth that we ought to be careful how we go about to destroy any *natural* product? You can build a tower "whose walls may reach to heaven" in a shorter time than you can cause an acorn to grow into an oak tree. On the other hand, how easy to destroy the oak tree! Now, certain things connected with society are— though you don't see the fact, and I cannot stop to give proof —analogous to the growth of a tree, *not* to the building of a tower. Can you, I may ask, attract back to Ireland the capital which has left, and is leaving it? Can you, by *any possible* "measure," make contract valid all over Ireland? Can you, *by any measure*, make one Irishman trust another? Can you make towns in Ireland pros- perous—towns I could take you to see—towns with shops—but shops *without customers*—shops in which, twenty years ago, you had to wait a considerable time before you could be served? To come to a personal matter, can you induce *me* by your "measures" to restore to Ireland the capital *I* have removed from that (artificially) wretched country? No! But I will tell you what you *can* do (nay, *have done*) by your measures: You can *banish* capital, *an- nihilate* contract, *put an end to* all confidence between man and man; and make the (hitherto) kindly Celtic folk around me, and who live upon the labour I give them—you can make them scowl upon me as if I were their tyrant and enemy, instead of their friend and benefactor![1] *That* you have done. Confidence, kindliness between man and man, you have put an end to. You have cut down *these* trees very effectually; but should you, after your operations on the trees at Hawarden, call together your friends and neighbours and, in their sight and to their ringing cheers, wave your axe and (this—your great "healing" measure!) order the trees you have cut down to wave once more in the breeze—you would not be engaged in a bit of folly more stark than you will

---

[1] I am happy to say that so far as the writer is concerned, the *I* here is only rhetorical. But how many worthy men in Ireland could with truth employ the form of words I have used in the text!

be, when you introduce (doubtless amid "loud cheers") your three "great" and "final" measures for "settling" the Irish Question.

In a word, civilized society is, in the greater part of Ireland, at an end *through your activity;* you have occupied about twenty years in the work, and you have performed it very effectually; now, when things are grown intolerable, you are, as I have before intimated, about to set them right by a more full and fatal application of the "measures" which brought them to this pass! —and all is to be done as by a wave of a magician's wand!— whereas, in truth, the soundest measures, were they devised by the very genius of enlightened statesmanship itself, would require many, many years before a bud or blossom of prosperity would attest the wisdom of the means employed!—But, coming to 'practical" matters, what would sound statesmanship say as to all that can be done in respect of the three measures you have undertaken to propose?—When we have ascertained this, we shall be able to judge of the soundness of *your* proposals—whatever they may be—when you come to make them.—

in regard to: (1) In regard to SOCIAL ORDER.—Remarking the curious
—(i.) Social —the significant—fact that a career of mischief which began by
Order; removing the "sentimental" grievance of an Established Church —the "Upas tree"—finds itself, in the end, confronted with *Social Disorder*—for that is what your measure implies,—I go on to say (speaking in the name of true, sound, scientific statesmanship) that this—"social order"— is the very point to which you *ought* to address yourself. You have, at any rate, *the right sow by the ear.* And all you can do is to *set in the right way again*—a thing which you have, for years, been exerting yourself *to force out of the right way.* You *must*—though you should lay Ireland in ashes (you won't have to do it though) from Fair Head to Kinsale —throw all the weight of English authority into the scale against systematic robbery *by form of law*—robbery as insolent and unjust as anything known to human history. This legalised robbery you have yourself established by your various *acts of justice.*—Then again, you must put down the robbery and violence which, as a necessary consequence, have followed your " *acts of*

iustice.[1] That is what statesmanship prescribes. Ireland will never see one bright day till Property, Contract, Good Faith come again to have some meaning for her inhabitants.—The abolition of these things and their passing out of the region of *the intelligible* is due *solely to your activity.*

(2) As to LOCAL "SELF"-GOVERNMENT: Sound statesmanship affirms that Ireland has no more need of any change in the matter of local "self"-government, than a cart has for a third wheel. The cry for Home Rule is a mere sham. It is got up by the Celt, in order that he may achieve his wretched " independence "—which would be fraught with destruction for him, as I have already shown,—but also, which is the only thing sound *English* statesmanship concerns itself about — for the peaceable law-abiding inhabitants of Ireland—of whatever race or religion,—as also for the very existence of England herself. The thing is not to be mentioned in your approaching Revelation, if you would avoid disaster to yourself and your country. You must not so much as *name* a Parliament in Dublin,—nor must you propose County Boards ; in short, you must eliminate this proposal from your programme of "measures" altogether. (ii.) Local Government;

3. As to the LAND QUESTION : Sound statesmanship would (*a*) avoid a certain highly-applauded course ; and (*b*) adopt a certain other course—which would startle most people.

(*a*) Sound statesmanship would never be so foolish as to dream of "rooting the peasant in the soil" by any process or means whatever. Apart from the fact that government has nothing to do with such processes, which are, in the very nature of things, totally independent of State control, sound statesmanship, in mere kindness to the peasant, would not, if it could—would not attempt to root him in the soil. The thing is, *even in conception,* a cruelty. Progress—civilization implies the power of the human being to move about over the surface of the planet till he find a suitable habitat.

---

[1] In Heaven's name, how can *you* blame, still less, *punish* moonlighters for committing outrages on those whom your brigand-commissioners have condemned to lose *one-third* of their property? *Can* you not see the argument of the moonlighter ? "The Court has reduced our rent by so much. But we have been paying this rent for *twenty—fifty—years.* Ought we to keep measures with such a ruffian as our landlord ? And if the Court grants us *one*-third, why not *two*-thirds, *three*-thirds?"

Men are not like oysters, which, when once they come to an anchor, never move again. But who can speak with patience of the presumptuous ignorance of those who would employ the money of the British taxpayer (*suppose the thing were feasible*) in " rooting the peasant in the soil "—in other words, in making an *agricultural* community of a people which has no talent, no taste, no gift for agriculture,[1]—and this in a country with an average rainfall of 208 days in the year![2] I wish sansculotte-christian-humanitarian statesmanship would concern itself a little more with *facts*, and very much less with fictions, dreams, and *doctrinaire* theories! This sort of statesmanship would " root the peasant in the soil " of Ireland?—Yes, very effectually in the soil—*but beneath the surface.*

(*b*) Sound statesmanship, in taking up the Irish Problem at its present all but insoluble stage would, as a first step towards solution—would, out of the Imperial Treasury (*not from Irish taxation !*) compensate to the full—as far as money compensation could—those landowners whose rents have been reduced by your brigand-commissioners. "*Public faith*" must be "cleared from the shameful brand of *public fraud*" if prosperity is ever again to visit an island whose troubles—of late years, at least—are *solely* the result of presumption, ignorance, cowardice, and shameless profligacy in those who stand forward as the special friends of humanity in general, and of Ireland in particular.

But, it may be objected, there would be great discontent in Ireland if this were done ; there would be disturbance—perhaps bloodshed. To which I reply : Real statesmanship is not bound to consider what the results of *healthy measures* following years of sham-statesmanship would be. Bloodshed, outrage, crime of all kinds *might* follow—they would, however, be the result not of the sound, healthy statesmanship but of the *sham* statesmanship.[3]

---

[1] This must be insisted upon. *The Celt dislikes Agriculture.* He has no aptitude for it. Are you aware that he never could be induced to cultivate *flax* which alone—in good seasons—could yield him adequate returns? What do you think *now*, good sir, of all your Land Acts?

[2] In thinking on such facts, of which I have had years and years of experience, I often ask myself, on reading such propo als as yours have been, "*Do we live in Bedlam ?*"

[3] I may ask in passing : Have you considered what the results, in respect of outrage, will be, should your "proposals" be rejected by Parliament and the

" But Parliament would not sanction such a measure." [1]   Did I
say it would?   Is not this an ideal sketch?   Would such a
statesman as I have imagined obtain a score of votes in any
constituency in England?   Have I not said that saxon England
would not *allow* such a man to see the light of public life—not to
speak of public official legislative life—for one day?   And suppose
him in your position, have I implied that Parliament would support
him in his activity?   Have I not implied—is it not one of the
main assertions in this letter—that the Parliament which *you*
have given us is incapable of settling this or any other public
question?   Is not the whole head sick, the whole heart faint?   Do
your constituencies know the Irish or any other question of public
importance?   Again, has the herd of candidates who solicited
their vote—their newly-thrust-upon-them "*right*," any opinion—
any knowledge—in regard to the Irish or any other question?
What was the burden of their howls before the crowds of "the
enfranchised"?   " *Down with wicked Tories! rack-renting landlords! grinding capitalists!   Allotments for the agricultural
labourer.*" [2]   And what do the candidates that were *chosen as
delegates* know about it?   Do you think I could for a moment
expect that sound statesmanship would be approved of by *such*
a body—representing *such* a constituency?

No: "Parliament would not sanction such a measure."   And
yet what I have stated is all that Parliament, that you, that anybody else, can do.   Then, when you have done what I have said—
when you have established order (were the process to cost a
hundred thousand lives), [3] when you have for ever given up your
mad project of tampering with natural arrangements—of rooting
the peasant in the soil, and when you have, *as far as in you lies,*

country? Outrage *for the present* has ceased. Are you aware that Outrage, having
hitherto been always successful in shaping your "great measures," but waits
to see what the parliamentary fate of your present "measures" will be?   But
is not that a strange predicament which the "Imperial" Parliament has got
itself into?   It legislates under terror of the ferocious and cowardly moonlighter
—his mask on, and his finger playing with the trigger of his revolver.

[1] There it is!   *Of course* Parliament wouldn't sanction such a measure!

[2] Every cry (observe) breathing the predatory spirit!   Not a vestige of
political perception left !

[3] The process would cost, in presence of a *worthy England*, very few, *if any*
lives !

indemnified the landowners for the losses which you have wantonly inflicted on them, then you may claim *Justice* as *your guide*. Were you my ideal statesman you would have to do something else— YOU WOULD HAVE TO WAIT. But having done *the right thing*, you would be able *then* to follow the policy implied in the petulant question of the Whig statesman, " Can't you let things alone ? "

This, however, is not the era of well-weighed activity and judicious repose. This is the era of vulgar sensationalism in politics ; this is the era in which the clamour is heard that " something must be done "—and *invariably* we then proceed to do the wrong thing—the wrong thing—which necessarily involves loss and suffering to millions. This is the era of " heroic " legislation. This is the era of the extinction of Parliament save as a pre-datory organization—this is the era of *one man* government. Finally, this is the era in which the destinies of the British Empire have been placed in the hands of the bitterest foes of the British Empire. *And therefore*, this is the era in which *the Irish problem passes into the region of things insoluble.*

What we—the English people—have before us, and how we are to manage with a Parliamentary machine that won't go, or go only for purposes of mischief, to our ruin and destruction as a nation and as individuals—these are questions which need not be discussed *at present*. I merely note that we have arrived at that pass at which we must embrace Revolution if we would stave off Dismemberment.

You are now, sir, so busily engaged on your great measures that you will in all probability fail to find time to read these remarks. Well, industrious, absorbed though you are, your proposals will one and all *fail* to settle the Irish Difficulty. And by how much they fail to settle the Irish Difficulty, by so much will they hasten the downfall of the British Empire.

I have the honour to be,

SIR,

Your obedient servant,

W. HART WESTCOMBE.

April, 1883.

P.S.—When I hear your proposals, I may have something more to say.   W. H. W.

APPENDIX.

NOTE A.

HERE are Worsaae's own words. After a masterly handling of *facts*—he concludes (*Minder*, p. 435):—

Det er saaledes ved de meest forskjelligartede Kjendsgjerninger fuldstændig beviist, at Normændene i Irland i mere, end tre Aarhundreder levede med egne Sæder og Skikke og under egne Bisper og Konger i Irlands vigtigste Byer, som de tildeels beherskede lige til den engelske Erobring (1170), at de vare de Förste, som i Irland *slog Mynt og drev nogen större Handel og Söfart*, og at endelig deres Efterkommere endog i stort Antal vedbleve at holde sig i Landet, selv efternt dette forlængst var erobret af Englænderne. Ingen Upartisk vil derfor nu kunne nægte, at Ostmændenes Bosættelser i Irland, som begynte med hyppig *at ödelægge Kirker og Klostre*, endte med i det Væsentlige at blive særdeles heldbringende for Landet, idet de ved Handel og Söfart af en tidligere ikke kjent Udstrækning först ret aabnede det afsondrede Irland for livlige. Forbindelser med det övrige Europa saavelsom med den der stadig fremskridende Dannelse. De af Östmændene meest besatte irske Byer, som ogsaa senere ere vedblevne at være Hovedoplagstederne for fremmede Varer og fölgelig tillige Midtpunkterne for Samquemmet med fremmede Lande, kunne med Föie siges noget nær at skylde Östmændene det egentlige Grundlag for deres nuværende Störrelse, Velstand og Magt.

NOTE B.

"Intelligence from Stornoway states that a shooting-lodge in course of erection at Drovnish Bay, island of Lewis, had been totally destroyed by crofters. The building, which was intended for the use of the tenant of the Scalisero shootings, was ready to be roofed. The contractor had occasion to go to Stornoway last week, and on his return he found the house razed to the ground and the materials scattered and rendered useless, all the woodwork being smashed. The crofters' interests were not being prejudiced by the erection of the buildings."

NOTE C.

Of course it is not the business of journalists to go back to first principles.— By the way, I must express my admiration of the articles which have appeared of late in the leading London journals (*Times, Standard, Daily Telegraph, Saturday Review*, &c.), on the Irish Question. Your own thurifer, the *Spectator*, has given you excellent advice; and you could not do better than follow the doctrines consistently maintained by the *St. James's Gazette*, provided you could devise some means whereby the *precious balms* of the Editor of that journal would be prevented from *breaking your head*.

www.ingramcontent.com/pod-product-compliance
Lightning Source LLC
Chambersburg PA
CBHW030537270326
41927CB00008B/1422